STORIES 𝄞 MUSIC

Volume 2

Stories of Music, Volume 2 - published in 2017
Published by Timbre Press LLC
Library of Congress Control Number: 2016921293
ISBN: 978-0-9969327-4-5 (pbk)
ISBN: 978-0-9969327-5-2 (companion web edition)

Cover design by Mercedes Piñera
Typesetting / interior design by Holly E. Tripp
Compiled and edited by Holly E. Tripp
Printed by Frederic Printing

Timbre Press LLC, P.O. Box 201435, Denver, CO 80220, www.timbrepress.com.

Printed on acid-free paper.

10 9 8 7 6 5 4 3 2 1

STORIES of MUSIC

Volume 2

Edited by
Holly E. Tripp

Foreword by Jeff Campbell,
founder of Hungry for Music

timbre
press //

"Music is the universal language . . . it brings people closer together."

- Ella Fitzgerald

Contents

TRANSCENDENCE

GHOSTS

Suggestions for Enjoyment of This Book

Stories of Music is a multimedia book, and the stories that follow sometimes include audio or video components. These can be accessed by using QR codes and simple URLs provided throughout the book that will direct you to the companion web edition (supported by all modern browsers). So that readers have easy access to the web edition, it is free and open to anyone. For this reason, it only includes the digital content and a couple other select works from the print book (for previewing purposes). Print readers have access to all of the stories.

Using QR Codes

It is recommended that you download a QR code reader app for your mobile device if you do not already have one (search for "QR code" in your app store and you will find there are several that are free to download). QR codes are provided for stories that include audio or video. Using your QR code reader, simply hold your mobile device over a QR code within the book. Once the code is scanned, you will be directed to the same page within the web edition, where the multimedia work can be played.

Using Simple URLs

If you choose not to use QR codes to access the audio and video content, you will also find simple URLs that you can manually type into your web browser (on your mobile device or computer). These will also direct you to the same page within the web edition where the multimedia work can be played.

Navigating the Companion Web Edition for the Best Experience

The user experience within the companion web edition was designed to be very intuitive. From your mobile device, you can simply swipe, or tap on the arrows at either side of your screen, to flip through the pages. You can also pinch to zoom in and out. On mobile devices, it is better to use the landscape position for the best viewing of photographs. This keeps photo spreads (where a photo takes up two pages) from being cut off. Also, because audio and video pieces only play within their individual pages, the landscape view allows you to see two pages while playing these works, so you can enjoy more of the story at once.

For the same reasons as listed above, it is recommended that readers who access the web edition with their computers also use the spread view; see the web edition menu items on the top-left of any page, and then click on "single-page mode" to turn the single-page view on or off (look for the icon that looks like an open book).

Foreword

There is irrefutable scientific evidence that we are all connected. Connected to nature and each other. Unfortunately, many of us cling to an illusory belief of separateness within our personal perceptions.

As we humans evolve and wake up to the fallacy of our separateness, it is music that is assisting in waking up our collective consciousness. Music's ability to heal, to communicate peace, to express love, to inspire change, to build community, and to give hope is helping to enlighten and open us up to a more harmonious existence.

You may scoff at the idea of a harmonious world, but the storytellers in Holly Tripp's multimedia anthology series, *Stories of Music*, give us hope that it is a real possibility. Holly's compilation of stories is a beautiful example of music's magical qualities that can help mend an ailing world.

I am very grateful to Holly for including Hungry for Music as a beneficiary of this wonderful anthology series and look forward to future releases as we musically evolve towards peace within.

Jeff Campbell
Founder & Director, Hungry for Music
Washington, DC

Preface

If you have read *Stories of Music*, Volume 1, you may already know how this anthology series came about. But, for those who are reading Volume 2 first, I'd like to share a bit about the project's beginnings.

I first became intrigued with people's musical experiences when I read my great-grandmother Gwendolyn's autobiography, *From Alpha to Omega*. In it, she described growing up in rural Missouri in the early 1900s and how local fiddle players would frequently entertain the community. I didn't find this at all unusual, but what caught me by surprise was that when the weather was too bad to gather in person, the fiddlers would play their music through the telephone party line. Folks would simply take their phones off the receivers and listen in; it was like a form of radio for them.

Gwendolyn's story prompted my curiosity about how people experience music, as did some experiences of my own.

I come from a very musical family. Growing up, my siblings and I enjoyed regular bedtime performances from our parents, who would play guitar and sing us some of their favorites: "Brown-Eyed Girl" by Van Morrison, "Teach Your Children" by Crosby, Stills, Nash & Young, and "Danny's Song" by Loggins & Messina, to name a few. My siblings and I would sing along, and frequently, we would make up songs of our own, albeit they were silly songs created merely for our own amusement.

Us kids learned various musical instruments over the years—some of us stuck with it, some did not. Regardless, we were connected through music, especially my brother Brandon and I, and we continued playing guitar and singing together into adulthood. When he unexpectedly passed away in a car accident in January of 2008, I was devastated. It was through music that I was able to cope with losing him. I continued writing music over the years, and in 2008, after Brandon died, I wrote several new songs that he seemed to inspire. I enjoy playing those songs still, but I'm most grateful for the creative nights I spent writing them because it felt like he was with me, encouraging me to keep making music.

The impact that music has had on my family and me led to the idea for *Stories of Music*. I wanted to learn how music was affecting others, to experience accounts of music changing lives. To find these stories, I put out my first call for submissions in early 2015, tapping into writing and art communities worldwide. By the submission deadline, I had collected more than 1,000 works for consideration—from stories of using music to reunite people after war and teaching music to prison inmates to learning to cope with depression through music and experiencing other cultures through their musical traditions. Story after story arrived in my inbox, and I realized I would be compiling more than one book. I received nearly 1,000 submissions again in 2016, in preparation for Volume 2, and I have no doubt this trend could go on forever because music truly touches people and changes lives.

As part of creating the *Stories of Music* series, it was also important to me to support nonprofit organizations that are increasing access to music. I have been inspired by the work of two organizations in particular: Hungry for Music, which donates quality musical instruments to underserved children with willing instructors and a hunger to play, and Music & Memory, which brings personalized music into the lives of the elderly or infirm using digital music technology. Both of these organizations are making a global difference, spreading the joy of music to those who need it most. To give back to their efforts, I am donating ten percent of proceeds from the *Stories of Music* books to Hungry for Music and Music & Memory. Your purchase of this book helps me to do this, and I invite you to support these organizations further by visiting their websites: www.hungryformusic.org and www.musicandmemory.org.

Music, I am learning, is rooted even more deeply in our lives—both individually and collectively—than I ever imagined. I have been overjoyed to discover how people are experiencing—and celebrating—music's many gifts. Little did I know when I began this effort that it would take on a life of its own because, I think you will agree, there's no end to the power of music. I hope I can continue bringing you these uplifting stories for years to come.

Holly E. Tripp
December 2016

Introduction

People need music. We crave it like nothing else, and its undying imprint on our lives spans generations and extends across cultures around the globe. Some might contemplate how humankind came to know music for the first time, or even how a song is born; some find solace in connecting with other people through music while others hold their memories in music. It's not always easy to explain our individual relationships with music, but one thing is certain: it has the power to bring us together. And in a time of astonishing turmoil occurring all over the world, I'd say we need it more now than ever before.

The power of music is what keeps the stories coming in for this book series, and as grateful as I am for the opportunity to experience these works, I am overwhelmingly proud and excited to share them with all of you.

The works presented in *Stories of Music*, Volume 2 not only celebrate music's remarkable place in our lives, but also how music can propel us forward—despite obstacles, pain, and uncertainty—and in some cases, save lives. The stories that follow demonstrate how music gives us a space to explore emotions we can't otherwise express, how it can open the door to new opportunities in life, and how it can become the vehicle through which some people transcend expectations. You will meet a host of incredible people in this book—legends known to a small few and some who have achieved great musical accomplishments and are celebrated around the world. You will travel back in time to experience monumental moments in music history, and to present-day India, France, Belgium, the United Kingdom, Israel, Russia, Siberia, Morocco, and the United States, where you will discover stories from authors and artists who continue to live through music today.

Similar to how the stories were presented in Volume 1, *Stories of Music*, Volume 2 traces our lives with music. This volume focuses on a group of themes that capture perhaps the most poignant of our musical experiences: origins, interconnection, exploration, "against all odds," transcendence, and ghosts. These themes tie in quite literally to some works, and in a more abstract way for others, but I hope you enjoy this presentation. And, as the selections here were chosen for their universal nature, I hope you find yourself in these works—remembering fondly similar musical moments from your own life.

ORIGINS

Tribal Rain Dance to the Beat of the Drum

by Francisco Parado Buenafe

Performers participating in the annual Sinulog Festival in Cebu City, Philippines give thanks to the Creator for bringing rain and vegetation to their dry land.

Dream Time

by Penny Harter

In Australia, the totemic ancestors walked across the land leaving words and musical notes in their footprints.
The aboriginals read the country as a musical score.

In the Dream Time,
the Ancestors went underground,
Honey Ant here, Wallaby there,
after their magic feet
had planted songs in the dust,

and by these songs, the people
learned each totem path,
singing the holy hillock, sacred spring,
and burning bush of their clan;
mapping kinship where the tongue shifted
but the song continued,
humming up from the underworld
like the first rivers.

When I listen to the whales
calling deep sea currents alive,
their repeating melodies answered
across great distances;
when I hear the wolves, the birds—

all the tribes descended from the Ancestors
learning the planet by ear, defining it by song
as the wind does each tree—
I do what I can,
throwing this song out from my house
like a rope in search of water
through the fire.

This poem was originally published in Penny Harter's book, Turtle Blessing *(La Alameda Press, 1996)*

Symphonious

by Patricia Belote

Beneath the boardwalk along Anderson Pond, the grasses grow
tall and golden, sustaining the direction of a south wind. It begins
at the far-off copse and rustles like distant timpani.   Near me
crescendo builds. All the grasses bow, their pizzicato prayer hands
plucking. And my own hair, a wind-blown grace note, plays along.
Softer breezes strum the water surface. Ripples trickle all the way
across.   Ascending, it sweeps through the forest canopy—
                        I hear it whisper a long time still.

Feels Wonderful to Dance

by Tommy Ballew

I was somewhere in my late twenties when my Dad invited me to accompany him to what would be my first pow wow. It was an encampment scratched out on a dirt plot north of Seattle. I obliged my Dad's invitation, but dragged along, wholly lacking the enthusiasm and enlightenment he was hoping for.

I grew up in Northern California, and my only exposure to Native American culture was the book *Ishi: Last of His Tribe*. It was required reading in high school; and, when it came to required curriculum of any nature, I had the resignation and oppositional disposition common to many high school students, and I was profoundly apathetic towards having to read this book. I might have begun my path towards early enlightenment had this book been shared with us in the passionate, inspired, reflective, and guided retelling that it so justly deserved. Sadly, it was assigned to us absent of color, context, or contrast to our contemporary Californian lives. I thumbed through it, wrote a detached book report, and that was that. It is my belief that the true story of our Native American forefathers is unforgivably left untold in our school system to this day.

To my enlightenment: I approached the encampment that day, and to my unexpected surprise, those drums . . . those voices . . . hit me

. . . dragged me in . . . sat me down, and shut me up. It was a baptism: the color, the groove, the swirl and twirl, the hypnotic trance-inducing pulse, the deep and profound centering, and the pulling together of all things beautiful. I was forever taken.

I go now, with great enthusiasm, every chance I get, to any pow wow nearby and, often, far from my home in Spokane, Washington.

I am, with sincere humility, a musician, credentialed primarily as a drummer. I do make a good go of it with strings and keys, as well. But, oh my . . . I genuflect to these tribal drums—these rollicking, rolling, and magnificent drums— and these bone-chilling voices. When I go, I sit studiously, captivated; I bob, jig and jag, tip and tap, and drift off into the realm of possible musical hybrids. As I listen to these amazing musicians, I can't help but want to jump right in, to play along with them, and to share these thoughts that I hear in my head. I syncopate with my feet and my hands. I hear other instruments joining the jam in my head that I, respectfully, hope might complement or possibly elevate it. So, that's what I set out to do with this recording.

The piece I am offering here is a labor of love that took me over two years to pull together, given the on-and-off time I had. Purists might argue that I have tainted a beautiful recording, but I pray otherwise. I have taken the recording of "Feels Wonderful to Dance" from the album, *Pow Wow People*—recorded by the extraordinary Black Lodge Singers—and layered upon it all those musings I have long heard in my head. In its purest, originally recorded state, the song features simply drums and singing. I used a porta-studio to, first, lay down this song as the foundation of my project. I then added two mandolin tracks— one to stay steady, and the other to wander—a cello, a pedal steel guitar keyboard sample, and a lap steel guitar, which I ran through a wah-wah pedal.

I wanted to capture—to ultimately evoke and convey—all that I feel, all that moves me, when I attend a pow wow: the power and majesty of it, the glorious din, the stirring of all the senses, from the thunder and lightning of the drums and voices, the cedar, the sage, and the sweetgrass to the blessings, the offerings, and the prayers. I hoped to honor the gathering and communing of kindred, collective souls in this piece. I wanted to take it upward, and then radiate it outward. I am contented that I have achieved what I set out to do, and eagerly invite you to listen and, hopefully, feel what I feel, in the way that I feel it.

I would like to thank the Black Lodge Singers of the proud Blackfeet Nation, who hail from White Swan, Washington, for their permission and blessings in allowing me my indulgences with their song. I would also like to express my wholehearted thanks to Tom Bee, owner of Sound of America Records, for granting me permission to utilize his recording of this song for my project, so that I may share it with all of you. Lastly, I would like to, lovingly and longingly, thank my dearly departed Dad for his invitation that day . . . a day which would eventually set the course for my journey and the creation of this offering.

Love and Peace,
Tommy Ballew

Scan to Listen

or visit
www.sombk.co/v2/11

"Feels Wonderful to Dance"
by Tommy Ballew
and the Black Lodge
Singers

"Feels Wonderful to Dance" used with permission from the Black Lodge Singers and Tom Bee of Sound of America Records

The Magic of the Mouth Harp

by Mukta Patil

It was a cool December night, nearing the end of the year, when I made my way to my usual Monday night haunt. Having newly moved to Goa, a small coastal state in India, this was one of the places I had discovered that had talks, live music nights, and movie screenings in my neighbourhood.

This particular Monday was to be a curtain raiser for an upcoming World Mouth Harp Festival of India, and several of the artists were to perform. My first thought when I heard this was, *I've seen a harp. It's massive, even larger than a person. How does that go into one's mouth?*

I went despite my misgivings, imagination running wild, absolutely not knowing what to expect. There were three or four people milling around the makeshift stage, with mics and speakers in place.

I am not one for exaggeration, but it was a night of magic. Three men took position and held something to their mouths, something barely larger than my palm. A girl later joined them.

When they started plucking away at whatever it was, moving their fingers faster and faster against their mouths, the sounds grew larger and enveloped me. It was a chorus of metallic vibrations, emanating from their mouths and reverberating in the air around us. A harmony of twangs changed pace and depth and duration to produce a glorious melody. It is not possible for me to describe perfectly what it sounded like—language is a poor substitute for the sound, and this, a disappointingly underwhelming description.

The three men were Sameer Thakur, Neptune Chapotin, and Rajesh Kotti. A girl hovered in the background, too shy to play in public. This was Amrita S. Anand. This is much more their story than mine, but mostly it is the story of a pocket-sized piece of magic that binds us all together.

***

The mouth harp has a story of strange origins, in that it doesn't have a clear one. A place in history is found for it in almost every culture and region of the world, and it is such a simple instrument that no one can really say for sure where it came from. It is known by over a thousand names, and it's played across the globe. It is called *mukkuri* or *koukin* in Japan, the *danmoi* in Vietnam, the *genggong* in Indonesia, *morsing* and *morchang* in India, *morchunga* in Nepal, *scacciapensieri* in Italy, *khomus* in Siberia, *vargan* in Russia, the *guimbarde* in France, and it is alternatively called the Jew's harp or jaw harp in English. It is impossible to say how many versions of the mouth harp are played in different parts of the world, simply for lack of documentation. There has, however, been a strong international resurgence of interest in the mouth harp in the past decade or so.

***

I had known Sameer for a few months then. A man of many interests, he is a theatre actor and director. He also runs a second-hand bookstore called Lotuseaters in Anjuna, when he is not working with his partner Arushi to consult with NGOs (non-governmental organizations) on sexual and reproductive rights.

His house is strewn with odd-looking musical instruments that he has picked up over years of travelling, and I have often seen him fiddling with them. "I haven't bought anything in a long time that wasn't at least a decade old," he once told me. So, it is only fitting that he would be interested in one of the most ancient instruments known to mankind. After listening to him play that night, I slowly began learning how to recognise the different kinds of mouth harps he owns.

Sameer grew up in Chennai, a coastal city in Tamil Nadu, and he first heard the mouth harp in music performances on television. The mouth harp forms an integral part of the classical Carnatic tradition of music practiced in South India and is often shown in televised

Mouth harps (photo courtesy of Neptune Chapotin)

performances. He picked one up on his travels in 2004, and has been playing it ever since.

His interest is not just in playing, but also in stories of origin, use, and style. The lack of information and documentation about the mouth harp is something that bothers him, and he hopes to start a project that maps the different kinds of mouth harps, beginning with India, and to collaborate with players across the world to trace the history, geography, and nomenclature of this ancient instrument.

Rajesh had a similar experience, his tryst with the mouth harp seemingly accidental but somehow preordained at the same time. For most of us who grew up in India, movies and television were the first and most prevalent sources of music. Rajesh's childhood was no different. In fact, when I pressed him to tell me about the beginnings of his infatuation with music and the long affair with it that followed, he attributed it to films. "I am given to understand that I was a big fan of Telugu films, and that I loved going to the theatre," he recounted. "Once, when I was two or three, I stood up and started dancing, and apparently people stopped watching the screen and turned to watch *me*!"

As for the mouth harp, his story began when he was in the sixth grade at a boarding school in Ooty. Like Sameer, he, too, heard it when he was very young at a live performance in school but picked it up himself much later in life.

In 2010, Rajesh quit his nine-to-five corporate job as a human resources executive and decided to travel for six months, which turned into a break of two years. That was when he walked into a music shop in Pushkar, Rajasthan.

"Understanding these musicians' beginnings is essential, because for a lot of mouth harpists, their journey is a lonely one."

When he saw the mouth harp, he knew it had something to do with music but thought it was a tuner or tool of some kind. When he asked the owner what it was, he took it and put it into his mouth, and a deep twang emerged. That was the moment he realised it was the thing he had heard so many years ago. In the beginning, he could produce only one sound—which is the stage *I* am stuck at right now—but he persevered and taught himself to play, which is what a lot of mouth harp players have to do.

Understanding these musicians' beginnings is essential, because for a lot of mouth harpists, their journey is a lonely one. Most of them have no community to look to—they learn on the fly through meeting people in their travels, or through online videos and tutorials. This is one of the reasons why the connections forged between this band of merry players in Goa and the community they have formed here is important—simply because it is something so hard to come by. Rajesh finally met other mouth harpists when he attended the first World Mouth Harp Festival of India in 2013, three years after he started playing.

This is incidentally also where he met Amrita, who he is now married to. He even proposed using a mouth harp! But, that is a beautiful story best saved for another day.

Perhaps the most ordinary tale of the lot, of how we became acquainted with the mouth harp, is Amrita's and mine. We both knew Sameer, and he introduced us to Neptune. Amrita and I are next-door neighbours. It is a small world after all.

On a summer morning we were sitting on her balcony. Though she claims to be an introvert, once she opens up to you, she can go a mile a minute, not unlike a train that has forgotten its stops. The sun was streaming in from behind her, lighting up the dark hair that fell loosely over her shoulders. She told me about meeting Sameer and joining up for theatre classes that he had started. Like me, she never quite paid attention to him playing the mouth harp until he introduced her to Neptune, whom Sameer had met at the end of the first World Mouth Harp Festival of India in 2013.

Since the festival is entirely participant-powered, Sameer offered to volunteer and roped in Amrita as well. That is how Amrita met Neptune, whose story I will come to in a minute. When Neptune realised Amrita couldn't play the mouth harp, he made it his personal mission to teach her, even gifting her her first mouth harp.

Which brings me to Neptune. He is a good keeper of his namesake's myth, born by the sea and in later years never seen without his own version of the trident, albeit a much smaller and more musical one. He was born to French-American parents who fell in love in the early '70s while traveling to India. His mother's love affair with the country ensured that her third child would be born in India, and that is how he came forth in Anjuna. In his early teens, they travelled back and forth from both France and the States until he was fifteen, and then they finally got one-way tickets to Goa.

When he was perhaps twelve or thirteen, he found an odd-looking object in a basket in his mom's room. Very thin, very long, three-pronged, with a little tail. He initially thought it was an apple corer, and remembers wondering, *but how do you get it into the apple?* When he finally asked his mother about it, she said, "Oh, it's a musical instrument. It's a 'juice' harp." And he thought, *oh, apple juice harp . . . but how does it work?* She then put it to her lips, and that was the moment his life changed and he became connected with the mouth harp forever. He says he can still remember the first time he made a

"As far as diversity goes, the mouth harp's is mind boggling. They can be classified not just by region, but also by makers, material used, and style of playing. The permutations are endless."

sound and thought *whoa, this is insane.* He was hooked—frame, tongue, and all. "At that point," he laughed and said, "this Beatles song called 'I Feel Fine' was stuck in my head. So, I basically taught myself to play the mouth harp by learning how to play the highs and lows of the intro to 'I Feel Fine.'"

Neptune was so taken by mouth harps that in 2001, he took a few back with him from Tamil Nadu when he went to the States, and people bought them. The next year he brought back a dozen of them to the States and sold them all to a local music shop. He eventually realised that it was possible to make a living doing something that he loved. Since 2009, he has been setting up shop in Goa, selling mouth harps at the flea market in Anjuna, and at the Saturday night market in Arpora. But his passion for the mouth harp goes far beyond just selling them. His intention is to share with people the tales of each mouth harp he procures from around the world and the joy and diversity these instruments provide.

As far as diversity goes, the mouth harp's is mind boggling. They can be classified not just

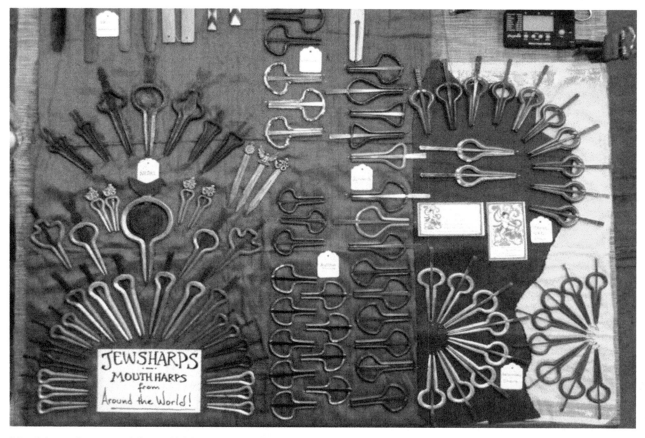

Mouth harps from around the world (photo courtesy of Neptune Chapotin)

by region, but also by makers, material used, and style of playing. The permutations are endless. When I asked Neptune about these distinctions he sent me a long email—a quick lesson that was part geography, part design, and part science.

"Mouth harps are essentially of two kinds based on design," Neptune wrote. "One kind is played on the teeth, and the other, on the lips."

The first kind is generally shaped like a tuning fork with a third prong down the middle; this central prong is pliable and is called the tongue. The two outer prongs of the frame are held tightly against the player's teeth; pressing one's lips gently down on the prongs creates an amplifying cavity. The tongue of the mouth harp is then plucked by the fingers to create vibrations that produce sound. The frames in this category are typically made of metal, either forged or cast—mostly iron—but can also be made of steel, brass, or copper. Wood or plastic can be used, too. The tongues are fashioned out of spring steel, which is often recycled from various sources like garage doors or clock springs, and sometimes even saw blades or umbrella spines.

The second kind is played on the lips and is crafted from a single piece of material—a flat strip of bamboo, brass, or even bone—and consists of a tongue carved out of the centre of the frame. Within this second category is another variation: the string-pulled mouth harp. Instead of plucking the ends of the instrument with a finger, the tongue and its vibrations are activated by pulling on a string, which is attached to the instrument, with sharp, repetitive yanks.

For both types, movements of the human tongue within the player's mouth provide modulation, and controlled quantities of breath are used to modify or intensify these modulations.

This explanation, though accurate, hardly does any justice to how the mouth harp resonates with a player. The feel of the iron against your teeth, the satisfying way that the tongue pulls out of your mouth as you release it, the way the inside of your mouth vibrates as a whole with the harp, and that sweet, sweet first twang as it emerges—these are all indescribable.

Different materials do, and will, produce different sounds. But the way one uses one's mouth also makes a world of difference. Since it has one tongue, each mouth harp can be tuned to only one key. Within this, based on movements of the human tongue and modulations of breath (whether from the throat, stomach, or diaphragm) the player can create different melodies. The fascinating consequence of this is that not only will each mouth harp have a different character, but the same mouth harp will sound different when played by different people, because each of our mouths are shaped in a unique way.

If I play a string on a guitar, or run a bow across a violin, and then you play it, and then a third person, it will mostly sound the same. But insanely enough, do this with the mouth harp, and each one of us will create a unique sound. "The really amazing thing about the mouth harp," Neptune said, "is that without you, it is nothing. Without using the musical instrument

"One of the first things people in the know tell me is this: you don't pick the mouth harp, the mouth harp picks you."

that is your voice, your body is not a musical instrument. When you place the mouth harp against your mouth and pluck it, only then does it make a sound. So you are, in essence, half the instrument." It is this intimacy and unparalleled sound that binds a person to their mouth harp. One of the first things people in the know tell me is this: you don't pick the mouth harp, the mouth harp picks you.

I was gifted my first mouth harp by Rajesh. He laid out four *morsings* in front of me and said, "Take your time. Play each one and see what they sound like. Feel the sound, and you will find the right one." And I did. Now I carry her in my wallet wherever I go.

Rajesh has given away over a hundred mouth harps like this, as gifts to people he has

"The rhythmic beating of the player's fingers against the tongue of the mouth harp produces almost hypnotic sounds that are trance-inducing."

met who seemed as excited about the mouth harp as he is. "Let the tribe grow," he chuckled in answer when I asked him why he does this.

For an instrument that is so very old, it sounds surprisingly electronic and new-agey. The rhythmic beating of the player's fingers against the tongue of the mouth harp produces almost hypnotic sounds that are trance-inducing. It is, therefore, not surprising that the mouth harp has deep roots in shamanic cultures around the world and is still used in shamanic rituals today. This element of it is what attracts Amrita to the instrument. She plays it for herself, interested in how the movement of her mouth, in conjunction with the mouth harp, produces vibrations that spread through her mouth and to her head. "I don't get high very often, but that is what it feels like when I play the mouth harp," she told me. "It does something to my head." When she is very tired, after a long day at work, she likes to sit back with her mouth harp until she enters a trance-like state—a calm and healing zone. Its ability to relax her is apparent when she plays, her eyes closed, face slack, arms loose.

One hot evening like any other in Goa, I went over to have tea with Rajesh and Amrita. There were mosquitoes everywhere, and the smell of incense floated in the apartment, doing almost nothing to dissuade the insects from buzzing and biting. Rajesh, however, was oblivious. He unzipped a case usually used to store sunglasses, and out fell a treasure trove. There were at least five different kinds of mouth harps that I counted. There were *morchangs* and *morsings*, a *danmoi*, something he called "Black Fire" from Hungary, and one from Nepal. And he played each one, demonstrating their differences in sound. Each was distinct, bound by its material and construction—some had more bass, others had a higher pitch, some were tinny, others more melodious, but all of them gorgeous.

Once he got into the groove, after the first twenty minutes or so, he even made sounds of water drops falling onto a roof and then a galloping horse. It was incredible to watch this magic unfold before me. Such an unassuming piece of metal, creating an entire universe of sound, was almost unimaginable until I heard it with my own ears.

I don't come from too musical a family, and my encounters with playing music have been few and far between, fleeting to say the least. A year of playing the violin when I was young was the closest I came to experiencing the joy of producing music. And suddenly, here was this man, kneeling behind me so I couldn't see him, but only *hear* the harp. Everything seemed still, except for the air around my ear. I could feel it vibrate as Rajesh breathed in and out, moving the tongue of the harp faster and faster.

This performance of sorts made it easier for me to understand what Rajesh had been trying to tell me about the experience of playing, about hearing it as if you were entering a universe that was becoming smaller and smaller, until you can see the atoms moving before you. After hearing Rajesh play, I became hungry for more mouth harp and decided to rendezvous with Neptune at the Arpora market, eager to talk to him and hear him play. I went for one mouth harpist, and I got three, because he had two young boys, Akshay and Jericho, who worked the stall with him.

Akshay was the more talkative of the two, and he launched into his story without much probing. The vibrations that the mouth harp makes in the mouth is what attracted him the most, putting him into a trance-like state of bliss. He has played the guitar and the flute, but nothing gave him the kind of goose-bumpy feeling of knowing something is just right like when he played the mouth harp. "The sounds of the harp just clicked into place for me. I broke the first harp I bought in two days because I played it nonstop," he said. Saturday nights were his favourite part of the week—the time when he could try different makes and models of the mouth harp and learn from the virtuoso himself, Neptune. Working at the stall, by his own admission, was one of the best things that had happened to him.

World Harps display table at a market in India (photo courtesy of Neptune Chapotin)

The Saturday night market at Arpora was a sprawling arena of stalls selling every imaginable thing. From spices to leather goods, food to silver, artefacts to designer clothes—ask and you shall receive. It was here that Neptune

> "He took the time to interact with the curious, guaranteeing that he could teach them to play the mouth harp in thirty seconds or less . . ."

had a small stall called "World Harps—Mouth Harps from Around the World." They started setting up at five in the evening, arranging the mouth harps that Neptune had acquired from his tireless travels all over the world. At last count, albeit it had been a few years before, he had about 4,000 harps in his collection. They ranged from 500 to 15,000 rupees, depending on where he had sourced them from.

The *danmois* were piled in a box, all in their multi-coloured bamboo covers. Arranged in concentric circles next to them were mouth harps separated by place of origin: Russia, Siberia, Germany, India, Nepal. In a glass box were the more expensive ones.

Very few people I saw on that Saturday night walked past the table without at least a double take at the shiny metal objects, so beautifully arranged. Children seemed especially fascinated by the display. There was an inevitable slowing down of the step as curiosity took over, especially if the boys were standing around, pulling at their mouth harps. "They are all different. They are all unique. They all have different sounds, different styles of playing," Neptune said to a young enthusiast, forgetting about me in an instant.

A basic lesson in playing was soon underway. "Hold it like this," he said. "Play it like that. Now try it while breathing in and out. Say 'A E I O U.' Great, now try it with a British accent, pulling at the vowels." In tandem, the boy whispered into the harp, eyes lighting up as the letters emerged in sound. At the back of the stall, I followed his instructions on my one-day-old harp, mirroring the boy's expressions of joy.

And on it went, the twings and the twangs of the mouth harp mingling with sounds of the market, a sea of music and mouths.

In this setting, it was clear that Neptune is a performer and people person, as he chatted easily with everyone who stopped by the market stall. At one point, he launched into a long conversation with a young woman from Assam, who enquired about the Bihu festival they have, confirming what he knew about the *gogona* traditions of Assam (*gogona* is what the mouth harp is called there). He took the time to interact with the curious, guaranteeing that he could teach them to play the mouth harp in thirty seconds or less, because once it is placed right, the sound production is a question of experimentation and practice. He was patient, a good teacher. He insisted that people satiate their curiosity, even if they didn't want to buy:

> *I've been running this place for six years now. And on an average, I've sold about five hundred harps every year. But for every harp that I have sold, there have been fifty or so people who I have taught to play, who have not*

bought it. So you do the math as to how many people I have managed to reach and introduce to this instrument, which is one of the things I had set out to do. And though I can't take the entire credit for the popularity it has now gained in India again, I can say that with the stall and the festival and performances, I have definitely played my part in it.

The World Mouth Harp Festival of India is Neptune's brain child and baby. It brings together artists and performers from all over the world, and the only stipulation to perform is that musicians include a mouth harp in their music. It is a mix of the old and the new, the traditional and electronic. For three days, people bask in the sounds of the mouth harp, and they feel the absolute pleasure of meeting others of their kind. It will enter its fifth year in 2017.

In between recounting stories of previous festivals and talking to all of his customers, Neptune told me more about his journey. Turns out he is also a performing artist, adept at the unicycle, juggling, and fire spinning. And that, for the last five years, since he was twenty-six, he had been traveling during the monsoon seasons to different countries to find mouth harp makers. He funded these trips by street performing in the different cities he visited, and then he used the money he had saved up to invest in new stock. This is how he had built up such a large collection.

"Each time I've met a maker, I've been really fortunate to sit down in their workshop and watch them make a harp," he exclaimed. Obviously my next question was whether he had ever tried to make one himself, to which he replied:

It's a dream of mine to make one. Because I now have the technical understanding of how they are produced. Not only how they are produced, but how they are tuned, how they are fine tuned, and the little tips and tricks that each of these makers have developed over their own experiences. So I know that the first time that I get a chance to make a mouth harp, or rather the first time that I would take a chance, I'm sure that it wouldn't be an excellent mouth harp, but I'm confident that it would make a sound, and it would make an okay one. I know what I'm working towards.

This is the kind of passion that drives him to explore as many facets of the mouth harp as he can. In 2011, he was awarded a medal at the International Virtuoso Competition held in Yakutsk, Siberia. (Apart from having the dubious distinction of being the coldest city in the world,

"It is a mix of the old and the new, the traditional and electronic."

Yakutsk is also known for its exceptional mouth harpists, as the mouth harp is their national instrument.) It was an honour that was well deserved, and anyone who has heard Neptune play would agree. He has spent years and years completely focused on perfecting his playing style, and he is a master of the craft. "I have always been like this," he said, "working on something I love until I perfect it. I was like this with my unicycle—I would never get off of it—then with the mouth harp, and with other passions along the way."

His hand is a blur of motion when he plays, and in profile you can see a part of his mouth vibrating where his fingers touch his face. That is all he needs to transport people into a heady zone of his beats. "I feed off of the energy of people. When I see people responding to my music I feel inspired to create and improvise," he added.

***

The questions I set out with, about what the mouth harp means to this small community of people I know in Goa, how they connect with it, and how they are experimenting with the sound, suddenly became intensely personal because of the nature of the mouth harp. And so the answers, in the end, have been deeply personal as well.

While Neptune continues his quest to find more mouth harp makers and popularise the instrument again, Amrita delves into her connection with the sound and what it does to her mind and body, Rajesh learns the intricacies of the sound, and Sameer journeys to map the mouth harp, I hope to find more people that it has touched in some way.

Till then, the fifth World Mouth Harp Festival of India will take place in Arambol, Goa, on the first weekend of February 2017, on the 3rd, 4th, and 5th. May the tribe unite.

Neptune Chapotin plays a Siberian Khomus from the Republic of Sakha-Yakutia with the setting sun in Arambol, Goa, India in March 2012 (photo and following video used with permission from Neptune Chapotin)

Scan to Watch

or visit
www.sombk.co/v2/23

"Sunset with a Siberian
Mouth Harp" featuring a
performance by Neptune Chapotin
(video by Darius Devas)

Learn more about the World Mouth Harp Festival of India at www.mouthharpfestindia.worldharps.com

Dulla-Bhatti

by Prerna Bakshi

"Sunder mundriye ho!
Tera kaun vicharaa ho!
Dulla bhatti walla ho!"

Catching me by surprise
my father sang
in Punjabi
on the phone when I called on Lohri—a harvest festival.
Excited like a young boy
whose Christmas came early,
he sang the folk song
that had been till then
resting on his lips
for years,
until one fine afternoon
it finally awoke
from siesta,
until it finally erupted
from his mouth,
like a ticking bomb that suddenly exploded
after, at the start, it failed to detonate.
Its first casualty: my virgin ears,
which bled in joy.

The sound of the long-lost folk song
pierced through my ears and into my soul.
When my father sang,
my every heartbeat danced
to the tune of "Dulla-Bhatti"
in perfect rhythm,
as if I knew it all along
even when I didn't.

"Papa, why did you never sing this song in front of me before?
Why did you never teach me?" I asked.
He paused, thought for a while and said,
"I don't know."

Post Partition, things never remained the same.
Though the wise old trees of Partition,
now divided, are to be found on
both sides of the border—
holding secrets of the unknown,
the many stories of a bygone era,
the horrors of humanity—
the roots of these trees
run deep.
Underground
they will intermingle.
And somehow, someway,
will find their way,
will find us, and
will not let us forget
our songs,
nor our roots.

This poem was originally published in Pear Drop *in 2015*

Tribal Dance with Musicians

by Chinmoy Biswas

This photograph shows a young girl performing a tribal dance with a group of musicians in Pushkar, Rajasthan, India.

Musicians at a Local Wedding

by Ata Mohammad Adnan

A group of musicians are playing traditional classical music at a wedding in Chittagong, Bangladesh.

INTERCONNECTION

The Language of God

by Robert B. Robeson

When my mother was ninety-one years old, and in a nursing home in Lincoln, Nebraska, I asked her to tell me about her life during the Depression. I wanted to document the early years after she graduated from North Central Bible Institute in Minneapolis, Minnesota in June of 1935, how she'd met my father—a minister—and the place music held in their lives. Some of her stories included events that I had never been aware of even though I was, then, over sixty myself. It would be a unique and insightful experience traveling with her down memory lane, and connecting my parents' passion for music to my own.

"Even as a small child in grade school," she began, "I had a desire to be involved in music, not yet understanding how important that would become to our later ministry in five states and in many foreign countries."

She said her parents had a pump organ and she used to annoy her mother by constantly picking out pieces of songs at home. She taught herself to play by ear, with no instructor, but finally learned to read music in high school choir.

"When I was a teenager," she continued, "I'd walk to our church after school, which was only a block from our house, to practice on that piano. In winter, in an unheated sanctuary, I'd frequently practice so long that I'd lose feeling in my fingers."

Her extended years and hours of persistent practice finally found an important outlet that began by word-of-mouth at the Lake Geneva Bible Camp in Minnesota toward the end of her high school years.

"Reverend Wesley R. Hurst, Sr., was conducting a tent meeting in Cokato, Minnesota," she said, "and someone told him about me. He asked if I'd assist them over the summer by helping care for their children and playing the piano for services. Even at this young age, I felt led to become involved in this endeavor. It was my first experience in active evangelizing."

During weeks of another summer when she was in Bible school, she assisted a brother and sister ministerial team with their tent meetings in Willmar, Minnesota. She played the French horn and piano, and also directed children's church. This began a lifelong interest and involvement in children's ministry.

When my mother graduated from the Bible Institute, she began looking forward to putting her knowledge and experience that she'd gained there into action.

Lois Grant, a close friend of my mother in Bible school, had attended a church in Sherburn,

Some of the musical and ministerial participants in a 1934 tent meeting service in Park River, North Dakota; from left to right: Lloyd Jorgenson, E.N. Oster, Helen Lockwood, Winnifred Gennow (Robeson), Myrtle Erickson (later Slater), and Mr. and Mrs. Louis Mudge of Bellingham, Washington (photo courtesy of Winnifred A. Robeson)

Minnesota. Her former pastor asked Lois to assist him in establishing a new congregation in Blue Earth. Lois, in turn, asked my mother to join her in this effort. During this era, store-front churches were spreading and springing up like marigolds in May. This pastor had been conducting street meetings in Blue Earth since 1934.

"Their faithful contingent used a large farm truck with a secured piano on its bed," mom said. "It was summertime, so they'd load the truck with church members, drive to Blue Earth, and hold street meetings on Saturday evenings."

Lois and my mother held eleven straight weeks of meetings at a building in Blue Earth. They took turns speaking and playing the piano as they assisted Reverend Byron Robeson, a young and single minister fresh from Bible school

"If I close my eyes and listen carefully, I can almost hear their voices, from almost seven decades ago, filling that small church with their joyous songs."

in Oklahoma. Lois Grant's former pastor asked Reverend Robeson to take over the ministry in Blue Earth. That's when my parents met. After a few months of courtship, they were married on November 29, 1935. Dad was twenty-four and mom was twenty-two.

My parents continued holding street meetings after that. They'd sing and play their instruments before dad spoke briefly.

In those days, the most effective advertising was word-of-mouth. Many people attended these services because it was one of the few things happening in small towns where finances and community events were limited. Since most people were affected by the Depression, most individuals had a need for personal and spiritual encouragement.

My older brother was born in 1938 and I was born in 1942, prior to our family moving to Truesdale, Iowa to serve in a new pastorate. Truesdale was a tiny hamlet of approximately 125 souls tucked away seven miles from Storm Lake in the northwestern part of the state. Even road maps barely bothered to notice it. This sleepy little town had a main street that consisted of one block of stores and businesses with a single service station across from a large grain elevator.

Though this church was so small it resembled a Holiday Inn room of today that had been forced through a compactor, each Sunday it was filled with seventy to eighty people, and often more. This equated to over half the town's population. I would sit on those hard wooden benches with my mother and, during song service, she'd use her finger to point out the words while the songs were being sung, which gave me a head start on learning to read. These folks, most of whom worked the land for a living, really loved to sing all of the old songs of the church. Most of them had the ability to maintain a positive attitude amid general climatic, physical, and often financial hardships.

I can still recall those hot and humid summer days before air-conditioning and indoor plumbing. As the services were underway and songs were being sung, there would be flies and bugs buzzing overhead with the aroma of hay and freshly cut grass wafting through open church windows from fields across the main road into town.

In one of my mother's photo albums, I discovered a black-and-white photo of the 1947 Christmas program in progress. A thirteen-piece orchestra is providing special music. My dad is seated behind them on the platform. The pews are packed and bunting is woven in and out of the platform railing. The lone light fixture above the platform has paper streamers draped to each side of the sanctuary. I remember these farm families joining in "Silent Night," "O Little Town of Bethlehem," and "Away in a Manger." If I close my eyes and listen carefully, I can almost hear their voices, from almost seven decades ago, filling that small church with their joyous songs.

When I was five, in 1947, two events occurred that made a deep impression on me. The first was when my parents took us to our first Blackwood Brothers Gospel Quartet concert in a larger Iowa town. Even from that tender age, I can still recall some of the songs they sang, some of the humorous things they did, and how magnificently Hilton Griswold, their original pianist, "tickled the ivories" with his magical touch. As we looked on from the first row on a side balcony, I remember everyone laughing each time Hilton spun around 360 degrees on his piano stool and came back without missing a beat. Nobody can tell me that music doesn't have the ability to make an impression on a person . . . even a little person. That night's quartet captured my heart forever.

The second event involved the death of a twelve-year-old cousin, named Larry, who tragically died of pneumonia in Minnesota. Death was not new to me because dad had other

Reverend Byron and Winnifred A. Robeson as newlyweds outside their first portable tabernacle in Blue Earth, Minnesota in 1936 (photo courtesy of Winnifred A. Robeson)

funeral services for church members in Truesdale that I'd previously attended. Yet, his seemed to have more staying power in my mind. Nearly six decades later, when his older sister and her husband were visiting in Lincoln, Nebraska, I asked her if she recalled the two songs that were sung at her brother's service. She couldn't, of course, because of her own trauma that day. But I could . . . and I don't know why.

"They were 'Sweet Hour of Prayer' and 'What a Friend We Have in Jesus,'" I told her. To this day, whenever I hear either song, my thoughts return to that 1947 funeral and it awakens deep emotion. This music will always be meaningful and special to me. A long time ago I recall that someone referred to music as "the language of God." Perhaps that's another reason those two hymns have touched me the way they have.

My mother encouraged my brother and me to sing together in church from as far back as I can remember, while she played the piano. We learned to perform before audiences in both small churches and large camp meetings during the summers while we grew up in a number of different states.

I began playing the trumpet in grade school in Gooding, Idaho. My brother had already been playing for years and he was probably an influence on what instrument I ended up with. From an early age, Jerry was really good and I grew to admire his talent.

By this time, even though our family was living a lower-middle-class standard of existence, our parents had invested much of their diminished finances into family instruments. My brother and I had our trumpets, dad played three different varieties of saxophones, the piano, and the musical saw, all of which he had taught himself. Mom played the piano, the accordion, the French horn, two kinds of guitars, and the ukulele. Music was a major part of our lives.

When our family moved to a new pastorate in Hoquiam, Washington, when I was beginning the seventh grade, my brother was in the high school band and I was in the junior high band. Once a month my parents led a city mission service in Aberdeen, in what many referred to as the "skid row" section of town. It was our twin city just across the river from Hoquiam, alongside Grays Harbor. I was often asked to play trumpet solos in front of these people who were down on their fortunes. I believe my parents wanted to expose me to the real world some people had to deal with, and to share my music and dad's message with those who seemed to have little of their own.

One evening after the service, and at a time when these visitors were being fed by the mission's staff, a transient and disheveled-looking man sat down at the piano. At first I thought he might be inebriated because of the way he walked, but this notion and narrative were quickly dismissed when he began playing a splendid rendition of "The Battle Hymn of the Republic." It was astounding to my junior high mind. I walked up behind him and complimented him on how wonderful it sounded.

He turned his head and, with bleary, bloodshot eyes said, "Son, use your musical talent for good and don't waste it and your life like I've done." I still haven't forgotten those words of wisdom.

When our family made its final move to La Grande, Oregon in 1957, at the start of my sophomore year of high school (minus my brother who was attending Bible school in Seattle), music and sports became what I lived for. My mother had become close friends with our church organist who was involved in a prison ministry at the Idaho State Prison in Boise. They often drove from La Grande to conduct services together there, with mom playing the piano, singing with her friend, and then speaking. I was brought along to play my trumpet and, I would assume, get a visual image of where I could end up if I didn't keep on the straight and narrow. This provided a different perspective on life I haven't forgotten either.

In my high school years, a continuous parade of musicians were featured in special meetings and services at our church. There were operatic Christian singers, country-western celebrity musicians, quartets, and all kinds of professional gospel talent who I was exposed to and able to interact with easily . . . because I was the "preacher's kid."

At school, I was in the band, mixed chorus, a mixed ensemble, and the boy's quartet. We were involved in a long list of concerts and provided free entertainment for a large variety of community and civic organizations. Our church also had a weekly Sunday evening radio program for the nineteen years my parents led the ministry there. One of my best friends, whose family also attended our church, was the lead singer in our boy's quartet and mixed ensemble at school. I was the baritone. We sang together on this program from our sophomore through senior years. In 1959, we were both selected for the 500-member All-Northwest Chorus that encompassed five states. This concert was held in the Seattle, Washington Civic Auditorium on Saturday, March 7, 1959 before over 20,000 people. I still have the press clippings, special patch, and 78-rpm record produced that night of the All-Northwest Chorus, Orchestra, and Band.

The chorus was conducted by Don Craig. We sang nine songs that included, in order, "Glory to God," *Ecce Vidimus* (Response No. 3), "Woe unto Them," "Soon Ah Will Be Done,"

> "I was brought along to play my trumpet and, I would assume, get a visual image of where I could end up if I didn't keep on the straight and narrow."

"Sing Me a Song," "Night Magic," "Open Your Heart to Spring," and "The Pilgrim's Song." It was a magical night never to be forgotten, even decades later.

During high school, our parsonage was always flooded with gospel music after my parents purchased a new stereo record player that had a permanent and prominent place in our living room. They would stack this player with a number of 78-rpm gospel albums as they went about their daily tasks. It was a way of life for them.

I played three sports in high school, but basketball was my favorite because of the close teamwork, camaraderie, and close fan support mere feet away from the players. The La Grande "Tigers" (our mascot) had an exceptional group my senior year. We tied with another conference team for the best regular-season record, 20-2, of the sixteen teams that played in the State Basketball Tournament at the University of Oregon in Eugene.

Giving our team a basketball, lighting and heating our home court on frigid December and January evenings in the Blue Mountains of Eastern Oregon, and providing loyal fans with a pep band playing "Tiger Rag," was a little like throwing Br'er Rabbit into the briar patch.

The newspaper clippings from that year are now as yellow as Homecoming mums. I still have the team pass and programs from that state basketball tournament. Whenever I leaf through

"A person only gets so many memorable musical moments in life."

the pages, it's Friday night again and I can hear "Tiger Rag" blaring in the background, making my adrenaline pump and goose bumps appear like they did then. Colorful twists of crepe paper flutter above the bleachers and the roar of the crowd sends shivers up my spine.

All of those basketball games remind me of what I'd been told is an ancient Tibetan aphorism: "It is better to have lived one day as a tiger than a thousand years as a sheep." Although I can't recall any schools in our conference with a predatory sheep for a mascot (or, for that matter, even in Tibet), I agree with what this anonymous and wise philosopher stated. And I'd wager he'd get a few goose bumps, too, if he could have heard La Grande High School's pep band belting out their version of "Tiger Rag" while raising the rafters of their "Roof of the World" before one of their Central Asian basketball games. A person only gets so many memorable musical moments in life. "Tiger Rag," in the land and lair of a host of tenacious "tigers," is one of mine that I'll never forget.

There were other special musical times, too, such as when our boys quartet sang our own version of the classic song of that era, "Moments to Remember," in the old La Grande Sacajawea Hotel ballroom for our senior banquet on Wednesday, May 18, 1960. I wrote the four verses about our high school days and sports activities that each of us sang or spoke individually, before bringing the full chorus together. I remember gazing out over that large audience and seeing my classmates, and even some of our teachers, reaching for hankies as we finished our high school days together. I doubt if I could ever recapture the emotion of those moments with my fellow quartet members in front of our classmates that evening.

A month before high school graduation, I enlisted as a medic in our local Oregon Army National Guard infantry unit, since the draft was still in effect. This began what would be an extended military journey that would ultimately find me living around the world on three continents. Music would continue to be a part of my life even still.

I went away for six months to complete my basic combat training at Fort Ord, California and then on to medic training at Fort Sam Houston in San Antonio, Texas. Then, a former high school friend and teammate, who went to our church, invited me to go to college with him in San Jose, California. We shared an apartment and attended college before being promoted to sergeants in the Guard. This meant we were eligible to apply for Infantry Officer Candidate School (OCS) at Fort Benning, Georgia in Columbus. Both of us were selected to go together after passing a series of tests.

During our final few weeks of training at Fort Benning, two other candidates in my barracks and I formed a musical trio. Both played guitars and had brought them along. When we weren't busy spit-shining our floors with Butcher's Bowling Alley Wax and our boots and shoes with water and rubbing alcohol, hour after hour, we'd find a quiet room and begin harmonizing. Other candidates would gather around to hear us attempt various songs, and they'd often join in.

One of our tactical officers overheard us singing one night and passed this word up the chain-of-command. Our company commander "ordered" the three of us to prepare two songs for a portion of the evening's entertainment at our graduation banquet. That evening, in front of a multitude of husbands and wives, dates, a one-star general, a colonel who'd won the Medal of Honor, and a host of other high-ranking officers and guests, our trio sang two songs. I don't remember what the first one was, but the final song was "500 Miles," which was popular in that

The late Col. D.W. Pratt, 95th Evacuation Hospital commander, presents Capt. Robert B. Robeson with his second Distinguished Flying Cross and second Air Medal with "V" (for valor) in early 1970 at Red Beach in Da Nang, South Vietnam (photo courtesy of Robert B. Robeson)

day. It told of being 500 miles away from home and lonely. Most everyone there could relate to it. We graduated in early 1965.

A few months later, my high school teammate and I were activated for a week, with our separate Guard units, in an effort to deal with that summer's Watts Riots in Los Angeles. A year later, my infantry unit was again activated by the California governor for three days during the Hunters Point Riot of 1966 in San Francisco. This would be the beginning of a long odyssey of devastation that I'd be involved in before the end of that decade.

After returning from OCS, I also had an opportunity to attend the first Blackwood Brothers concert since my first exposure to them in Iowa at the age of five, approximately

"It seems as though church and music have always been a positive influence in my life and have provided the greatest blessings possible."

sixteen years before. I'd collected many of their records through the years. James Blackwood, their lead singer, was the only member from the original group so many years before. But I was still thrilled, inspired, and enthralled with their music.

I met my wife, Phyllis, in a church in San Jose when she was in the choir and I was playing in the orchestra. It seems as though church and music have always been a positive influence in my life and have provided the greatest blessings possible. We've lived on two continents during my military career, and we continue to love music and each other after forty-seven years together.

In the late 1960s, my brother and his family became missionaries to Nicaragua and Costa Rica. He began a TV ministry there that reached a wide swath of viewers in Central America. He sang and featured his special trumpet playing. Later, he made a variety of vocal and musical recordings that I still have, along with private recordings of him playing and singing with my parents when they were much older in life.

With the Vietnam War beginning to heat up in 1968, I volunteered to become a helicopter medical evacuation pilot for the Army, and I spent ten months in flight schools at Fort Wolters in Mineral Wells, Texas and Hunter Army Airfield in Savannah, Georgia. I graduated as an Army aviator on March 25, 1969. Four days later, I was married. Three months later, I found myself in Da Nang, South Vietnam as a captain, a medevac pilot, and operations officer for the 236th Medical Detachment (Helicopter Ambulance), headquartered at Red Beach on the southern shore of Da Nang Harbor. Seven months later, I would be promoted to commander of the unit.

In that traumatic one-year tour of duty, I'd fly 987 missions, evacuating over 2,500 patients, would have seven aircraft shot up by enemy fire, and would be shot down twice.

I remember one mission in particular. It was the second time I was shot down and it occurred on Christmas morning in 1969 on Barrier Island, about twenty miles south of Da Nang near the South China Sea. Nine ARVN (Army of the Republic of Vietnam/South Vietnamese allied soldiers) had been seriously wounded and were surrounded in a tiny outpost. There was supposed to be a Christmas ceasefire in place, signed in Paris, France, but someone had forgotten to tell these guys shooting at them. Since we were constantly observing ravaged bodies, horrendous suffering, and destruction mission after mission, our crew members would often tune in to Armed Forces Network (AFN) radio on one of our three or four radios. Listening to music helped calm our spirits between missions. This was especially true for the eighteen to twenty-year-old medics and crew chiefs.

When I clicked my communications switch to AFN for a few minutes on the way to this grid coordinate, I was surprised to hear them playing a song by the Statesmen Gospel Quartet, with Hovie Lister at the piano. This was another favorite gospel quartet of mine, whose records I'd collected with those of the Blackwood Brothers long before my combat tour. James "Big Chief" Wetherington, their brilliant bass, was in the midst of a solo part in "Peace, Peace, Wonderful Peace." It was so out of character to hear gospel music on AFN instead of the usual pop and rock 'n' roll tunes that flowed from hootches and transistor radios back at our base at Red Beach.

As I made a high speed and radical combat approach toward the colored smoke grenade—tossed out by the ground troops to mark the landing area next to the wounded—enemy fire opened up on us with automatic weapons as we fell through 600 feet. We took nineteen hits in one fuel cell, the cargo compartment, and the cockpit. Miraculously, none of us were directly

hit, although our crew chief had his foot kicked into the air when a round made an indentation in the cargo deck where his foot had been. With fuel draining out beneath our jet engine exhaust,

"Listening to music helped calm our spirits between missions."

we barely made it back to a troubled landing at Landing Zone Hawk Hill, thirty-two miles south of Da Nang. We lost 250 pounds of fuel on that return flight. Transferring to a replacement aircraft, we returned to complete the mission. On our third attempt from a third direction, also under enemy fire, I was able to land and safely evacuate all nine patients to our battalion aid station. In the years since then, I've wondered if God might have used that quartet song at that precise moment to assure me that everything would work out in the end. Perhaps He wanted me to be at "peace" about it.

After the Vietnam War, our only child was born in West Germany at the Landstuhl Army Hospital, where I flew with the 63rd Medical Detachment as an operations officer, and later as commander. Music continued to touch an additional generation of our family when our daughter, Denise, was in high school in Lincoln, Nebraska. She was in a number of special singing groups that toured and won numerous musical competitions in neighboring states. Hearing her perform solo jazz scats in her high soprano voice in concerts and competitions, and singing renditions of popular Sandi Patty gospel songs in church and youth gatherings, provided me with additional awareness of how far my parents' love of music had touched our family. My only regret is that her grandparents never had the opportunity to hear her sing.

When my brother suddenly passed away at age sixty in Oregon, on September 18, 1999, after those many years as a missionary, six of his recorded vocal and trumpet solos were played during his funeral service. They were "In the Valley He Restoreth My Soul," "When They Ring Those Golden Bells," "I Am a Pilgrim," "He's Everything to Me," "I Wouldn't Take Anything for My Journey Now," and a final foot-tapping and emotional send-off featuring his version of "When the Saints Go Marching In." He left this world displaying his musical talent even past the ending of his own breath. Unlike many, he was able to perform at his own funeral.

My father's life journey ended at the age of ninety-one, in 2002, and my mother's at over ninety-five in 2008. They'd been married over sixty-six years. As my mother's body began to break down from renal failure, nursing home staff placed a tape recorder next to her bed, playing gospel tapes that were her favorites when she was still aware and coherent. I believe her subconscious undoubtedly enjoyed the music as she transitioned from one realm of reality to the next. I'm sure she appreciated it on the way to joining dad on the other side.

Today, I'm seventy-four years of age myself. I've found, as so many before me, that life is full of extraordinary experiences filled with surprises. Generations of Americans have survived the pressures, disappointments, embarrassments, and anxieties of life in the past century. I've learned in this living process that it's okay to be human. It's all right not to turn in an Oscar-winning performance every time in whatever we do.

The journey of each of us through life, the poet reminds us, can be a tale of adventure and discovery, menacing winds, enticing sirens, monsters within as well as without. But through the long cycle of generations, we press on living and dying, longing to find that moment when we understand completely who we really are and what we are able to achieve for ourselves and others. And regardless of how each one of our lives plays out, I believe we all become aware that it's easiest to endure if we do it with a song in our heart and soul. Perhaps that's why music is called the language of God.

In the Rehearsal Room

by Anna Alferova

As musicians gather to play, magic unfolds. Here is a glimpse from a trumpeter's view.

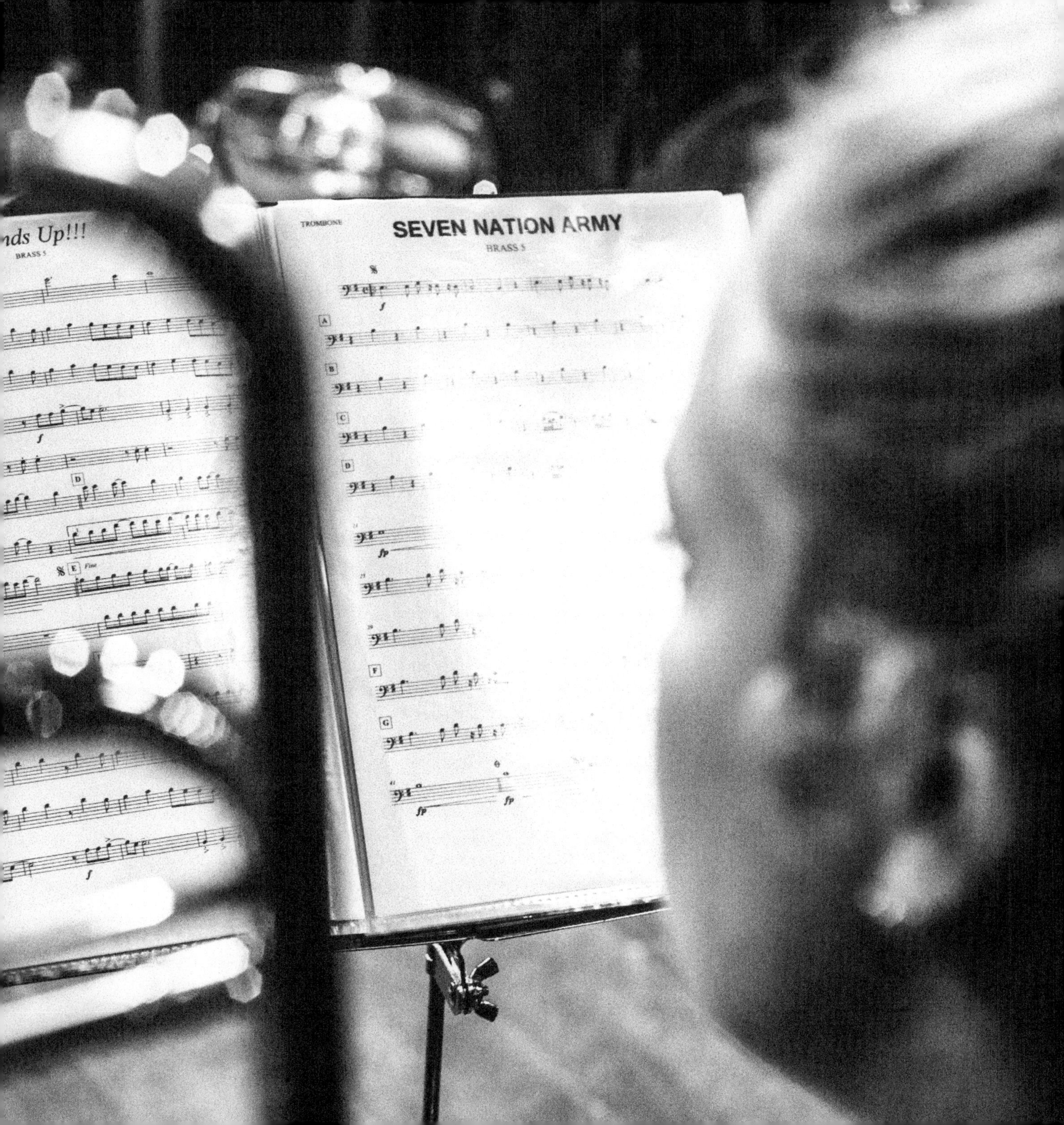
nds Up!!!
BRASS 5
TROMBONE
SEVEN NATION ARMY
BRASS 5

The Transatlantic Flute

by Pierre-Marie Bernard

On both sides of the webcam, everybody froze. Time itself froze, not quite sure of what was happening either. My father, Michel, shaking himself out of his immobility, was now leaning toward the computer, moving his arm and hand slowly in an attempt to catch the flute that his granddaughter seemed to be handing to him from the other side of the screen. From Belo Horizonte, Brazil to our flat in Lyon, France.

It was the day before we were going to put him in a nursing home. It was the last day for him in his true home, and his last webcam session with my little brother Frédéric's family—he, his wife Ji-Young, and their two children, Matteo and Youna—all of whom had expatriated to Brazil. The first minutes of this session had been filled with small talk, games, and dances by the kids in front of the screen. On our side in France, my brother Christian, my mother Jacqueline, my cousin Sonja, and I stood in a circle around my father, who sat, still, at the centre.

My dad had not uttered a single word since the start of the session, silent as he was too often. He had never been much of a talker actually, but illness had taken its toll on him. For the past ten years, Parkinson's disease had sprinkled his neural connections with rust, paralyzing them one after the other. In these conditions, every move, every word was exhausting, but a small victory for him. So, he often saved his few words to crack an unexpected joke, his own way to wink and wave at us. In spite of everything, and against all odds, he was still here with us, just in our periphery. It had been some time since his last wink.

Was he even aware that this was probably his last webcam session with us all? Probably not, judging by his apathetic behaviour and fixed stare. Until his granddaughter Youna grabbed her little plastic flute and started blowing into it with all the energy and air a five-year-old can gather in her lungs, which was quite impressive if you ask me. Then she came closer to the screen and held her flute right in front of the webcam so that we could all see it well. This woke my father up. He really thought she was handing him the instrument! In disbelief, we all watched him move his hand forward to grab this "transatlantic" flute, anticipating his disappointment, like when you uselessly close your eyes before your car crashes and everything seems to happen in slow motion. Well, fear does not eliminate danger, as we French say, and eventually, his fingers touched the screen.

A former alpinist, my dad was not one to be defeated easily, though. At least the disease had not altered that. He recovered immediately from the surprise and made a small gesture with his hand to the right. My mother understood right away what this was about. She opened a drawer and pulled out one of the flutes he kept there. He made another gesture to tell her silently that "yes" that was the idea, but "no" that was not the right flute. He had always been picky about his musical instruments. She then proposed another flute, which he grabbed as he gave us a large smile. That one was the real thing: a heavy, beautiful, brown wooden flute with a deep sound; he had brought it back from Brazil some fifty years before. All of this happened without a single word being spoken.

However, when he put the instrument to his lips, the silence became even thicker on both sides of the screen. I bet even the soft hum of the computer faded completely when he put his stiff fingers clumsily on the flute holes. He started to play a melody that we could not recognize. It didn't last more than a few seconds, just long enough for him to blow a dozen trembling notes. The last one hung in the air like a balloon slipping from a child's hand, and then took off and vanished. I don't know who recovered first, but all of a sudden everybody was clapping, the kids with their characteristic exuberance and the adults with heavy hands. My father then gently put the flute on the table, exhausted from the effort, and slowly left the room. He was followed like a shadow by my mother who was anxious that he might fall. Meanwhile, the rest of us grownups entered a throat-clearing contest that was conveniently smothered by the noise of the kids who went back to their business of being kids.

We didn't hear our father's voice during that webcam session, and maybe not even that whole day, but I believe he wanted to tell us

"I bet even the soft hum of the computer faded completely when he put his stiff fingers clumsily on the flute holes. He started to play a melody that we could not recognize."

something important with his short melody. His intentions are anyone's guess, but I felt it was his way to bring love to a family he knew he would be leaving soon. And, it does not come as a surprise that it took the shape of music since it was such a big passion in his life. He has since passed away. But, I cherish that Brazilian flute as part of my family history, and I always listen to his favourite tunes whenever I want to say *hello*. Like Celso Machado's "Pacoca"—all beauty and simplicity . . . something so light and pure that you can take it anywhere with you, hum in the shower, and whistle in the sunshine. Hearing that flute is like speaking with him again.

Fantasy for the Flute and Piano

by Elizabeth Erenberg

Scan to Listen
or visit
www.sombk.co/v2/49

"Fantasy for the
Flute and Piano"
performed by
Elizabeth Erenberg
and John McDonald

This piece was written by composer Russell Steinberg. To describe the song, he says, "The flute chants inside the piano, creating an aural resonance whose overtones unfold the harmonies of a mysterious chromatic landscape that ultimately evolves and pushes through to a world of tonal serenity. That is essentially the journey of my 'Flute Fantasy.'" This piece was performed by John McDonald, on piano, and me on flute, and it appears on my 2015 album, *ASCEND*.

Piano at Five

by Elizabeth Kirkpatrick Vrenios

Picture me: shy, hungry at the door
peering into the dark interior,
dog-eared Thompson's *15 Easy Pieces*
clutched to my gingham flat-chested dress.

Watch as I descend into the scent of old paper
and mothballs
to perch on a stack of encyclopedias,
Volumes A through E,
nobby covers worn smooth by so many
young bottoms sitting up straight
while the metronome ticked.

Here "Aeroplanes" and "Elephants"
lift me up to the keyboard,
my Buster Browns scuffing
the underbelly of the upright,
its dark mahogany skin
cracked and scaled like the rattlesnake
I saw my father kill in the field.

And nested on top of the piano,
pungent over-ripe bananas
curve over a crockery bowl,
bobbing time with my left-hand thump.

Watch as I lose my place and forget the tempo
in "Airy Faeries," doubting the metronome.
Ah! Those yellow wags,
chiding me for too little practice.

So this is what it comes to,
how it ends without ending:
Late afternoon nudges through the lace curtains
and slithers across the dark oriental,
and I hear the back-and-forth traffic
of laborers returning home,
the music of beeps and honks
mix with the ticks and tocks
I thump to,

never quite keeping the harmony.

Family Tree

by Gary Fearon

Scan to Listen

or visit
www.sombk.co/v2/52

An author reading
of "Family Tree"
with music

Growing up, it seems like music was always playing in my home. From as early as my two older brothers and I can remember, our Massachusetts childhood was filled with the sound of music.

My mother found playing the piano to be her greatest outlet. She played every day—in a grand old style filled with arpeggios and other embellishments—on an aging second-hand piano my dad bought from a church. In time, a nicer, new Wurlitzer took its place, its shiny black finish assuming center stage in the room my mother called "the parlor."

Parlor. That antique word still amuses me. Even today, I'm not entirely sure what the difference is between a parlor and a living room, which is what it was, but the atmosphere my mother created with her elegant playing definitely fit the more formal-sounding "parlor."

I myself dabbled with the keys a bit . . . only simple beginner tunes like "Chopsticks," of course. But I occasionally made up little melodies.

When the piano wasn't going strong, our big console stereo—also in the parlor—was playing the latest movie soundtrack. My parents took us to the cinema a lot, especially to see musicals, which were probably their favorites. I know they were mine.

My dad, by the way, was more artistic than musical. He didn't play an instrument, but he could sing. The first time I heard many of the old standards was when my dad sang them to my mother.

In time, my teenage brothers got guitars. My oldest brother Wayne had a Gibson flat-top acoustic, and Ron had an electric bass, a copper-colored Weiss. They became very skilled very soon through learning to play songs by the Beatles, Bob Dylan, and other artists of the day. Before long, my brothers were writing their own songs, creating quite an impressive catalog.

You could call them a two-man garage band, except for the fact that we had a cellar, and that's where all the magic happened. I'm grateful that we had a Webcor tape recorder in the house during those years to capture many of these musical moments.

These original songs became well-known in my family's large circle of friends. Any time guests came over, or someone had a party, they would ask my brothers to play. And of all the catchy tunes Wayne had written, one stood out as the signature song. "In a Tree" was inevitably requested. Friends knew it well enough to join in.

The annoying little brother that I could be, I wanted in on all this action, so my parents bought me a melodica. You don't see them around anymore, but it was a hand-held cross between a harmonica and an organ, sorta. I wasn't very good at it, finding its sideways keyboard harder to play than the piano. Plus, you had to blow into it, which for a kid with asthma was less than ideal! In any event, my brothers graciously let me horn in on their duo, and I regret that I ruined many of their recordings with my unmelodious melodica.

In time, Ron gave me some pointers on how to play bass (probably to get me off the melodica), and that basic education went a long way toward helping me learn to play guitar. When I got hold of the sheet music for my favorite Paul McCartney album, it included the guitar tab, and then I was really on my way. I inherited Wayne's flat top, now that he had a Gibson Firebird electric guitar.

These musical years came to a halt during a relatively short period of time during which my father died in an accident, my brothers got married, and my mother and I moved 1,000 miles away to live near her family. My brothers got into "legitimate" lines of work, so writing music fell by the wayside.

My new home, a small town in North Carolina, had a local AM radio station. I was a teenager, myself, at this point and would call the station to make requests. (This was back in the days when they took requests.) I got to know the program director, and one day a visit to the station found me getting hired as an afternoon DJ.

Spinning records—and getting paid for it—was a dream come true. And because this particular station played country music during the day, pop hits in the afternoons, and added blocks of bluegrass, gospel, and easy listening on the weekends, whatever my musical education had lacked up to that point was quickly filled in. To this day, I can tell you what year almost any song I played on the air was released, because I can still see the year written in bold letters on the face of the 45.

By this time, I had my own stereo tape recorder and, having gained a certain proficiency on piano and guitar, was writing and recording my own songs. I loved overdubbing and doing all the instruments myself.

Over the years, I continued to write—just as a hobby—while I moved up the broadcasting ladder from station to station, ending up in

"I like to think it would make my mother proud to know that she played a huge musical role in my life."

Memphis. Because that FM station hosted a lot of concerts, I even got to meet many of the recording artists I admired.

By this time, my mother had died in a drowning accident, and my part of her will saw me investing in professional recording equipment. Soon I was writing and selling jingles to radio advertisers, and recording more songs than ever. I like to think it would make my mother proud to know that she played a huge musical role in my life.

As the years went by, I added studio production to my resume. I created many song parodies for morning shows, selling them to comedy networks and national talk shows. Music has never *not* been a part of my life.

Throughout these same years, Ron reconnected to music, playing bass in several popular Boston-area bands. Wayne followed more of my father's path, in a career that utilized his artistic skills. His Firebird guitar was stolen

at one point, so music wasn't even an option for many years.

What little communication I maintained with my brothers amounted to a phone call once or twice a year, if that, and email exchanges with Ron that went in flurries . . . several in the course of a week, and then months would go by. That sounds a little weird and distant to friends of mine who stay in touch with their families, but for us it always worked. Plus, we're guys! We don't pick up the phone just to chat. We knew we would always be there if we needed anything.

Two years ago I got a phone call. I knew that Wayne's wife had been ill for some time, but the death of that dear lady still came as a shock. The private funeral had come and gone, so I didn't go, but the sad event triggered a surge of phone calls between my brothers and me. In our first conference call with all three of us on the line, we were surprised at how long it had been—twenty years—and how easily we picked up right where we left off. The biggest surprise was realizing how much it meant to us to reestablish our connection. When someone suggested we meet up in person, we were in instant agreement.

I love a good road trip, and they were ready for adventure, too, so we decided to take what was now 1,300 miles between us, divide it up, and meet halfway in Virginia a month later. Since Ron and Wayne live in adjacent cities, they'd ride together. We would bring our guitars and make a week of it.

In preparation, I gathered up as many of our old recordings as I could find and made

CDs for each of us to listen to on our respective journeys. I had a blast driving through the beautiful Blue Ridge Mountains, while Wayne and Ron enjoyed stopping at landmarks along their route, such as America's oldest drive-in theater. Along the way, the soundtracks of our teenage years only heightened the anticipation of our reunion.

Ron had made reservations for us at a hotel in Salem, Virginia. I arrived about an hour before they did, and explained to the desk clerk that I was there for a twenty-year reunion with my musical brothers, asking if there might be a conference room we could borrow to jam in. Although there was no such room at the hotel, the gal was accommodating and reassigned us a room that had some distance from those currently occupied, so we could at least make a little noise without disturbing others.

Seeing my brothers after twenty years was everything you can imagine. "Surreal" was the word we kept using. We couldn't wipe the smiles off our faces, spontaneous hugs were frequent, and our non-stop questions and answers and comparisons about what we remember enlightened us all at every turn. Wayne brought an enormous box of photographs and memorabilia from our childhood, and almost every one of them triggered an eye-opening story.

I was thrilled to learn that Wayne had started writing songs again, and he brought a guitar he'd recently acquired. Ron brought the latest in his succession of basses, and I had both my Alvarez guitar and a portable keyboard. We had come with great expectations, but between all our reminiscing, sightseeing, and trying local restaurants, we didn't find much time for music. Plus, we were still a little inhibited about making too much noise in the hotel. So we focused on just being together, and it was one of the greatest weeks of our lives.

So great, in fact, that before we parted, Ron and Wayne decided they would make another road trip in a few months and this time come all the way to my home in Memphis. Six months later, they did just that, and brought along Ron's wife and daughter.

Once again, there was plenty of sightseeing, eating out, and reminiscing to be done, but this time we did make music. I got to hear the new songs Wayne had written, and we jammed almost every day, playing everything from our classic originals to Burt Bacharach. Making it even more meaningful, we were often joined by my son—an accomplished guitar player, and Ron's daughter, who had brought her ukulele. It was satisfying to my very soul for two generations of our family tree to be making music together.

As we did decades ago, we had the tape recorder rolling. And of course, we had to do Wayne's signature song, "In a Tree."

My brothers and I have made something of a pact to get together every year if we can. This spring, Wayne and Ron will return for another visit, along with Ron's wife and daughter, and I can't wait. My brothers and both of my parents each have birthdays in the spring. When they come, we'll raise a glass to all of them. And once again, we'll make music.

Escape

by Elena Polyakova

A member of the Novosibirsk Philharmonic Orchestra is on her way to perform at the airshow in Novosibirsk, Siberia.

The Soul Doesn't Sleep

by Kelly J. Stigliano

She was very gracious when I got the job. When told that I would share her office, because we both worked part-time, her only concern was that I would find the small space too messy. She always promised to clean it up—someday. Being a bookkeeper, and a disorganized one at that, her piles of worksheets were important and couldn't be moved. I respected her little mountains of paper, and she made room for a framed photo of my family.

Brenda worked Mondays, Wednesdays, and Thursdays. I worked Tuesdays and Fridays. We communicated with one another by leaving notes beside the phone or on the computer monitor. When she had to work extra hours, I was moved into an empty office. I didn't mind because I loved the few minutes that we stole to chat.

She and her husband, Chuck, both of whom were in their sixties, lived alone on the other side of Raleigh. Their cats were their children.

Brenda was taking harp lessons. *Harp lessons? At her age?* Yes, it was something she'd always wanted to do and Chuck encouraged her to pursue it. She said it was a challenging instrument to learn, but that she found it relaxing.

Because Brenda was a private person, we were all pleasantly surprised when she and Chuck invited everyone, along with our spouses, to their house for a cookout on their new gas grill. Chuck studied the monster-sized thing, and eventually cooked steaks and chicken for us. We each provided a side dish.

I was amazed at the size of their house. No tours, though.

"It's too messy upstairs," she said.

What a wonderful evening it was—we finally had time to just sit and talk. Getting to know Brenda and Chuck was a delight. However, we later learned that we really didn't know them at all.

A few weeks after the cookout, Brenda and our boss had a disagreement in our shared office. I found out that Brenda had collapsed on our office floor, and Chuck had taken her home.

Within the week, he called to say that Brenda was in the hospital in a coma. *Why?* We were all astonished to learn that she'd been on a waiting list for a new heart. Her celebration of life and non-complaining attitude fooled us all into thinking she was healthy.

Our co-worker Nicole and I visited Brenda in the hospital. She was in a tiny room crowded with large electronic equipment that whirred, clicked, and beeped.

Chuck told us that Brenda's wedding ring had been removed when she entered the hospital.

That evening she had slipped into a coma. The following day, the hospital chaplain led Chuck in renewing his wedding vows to a comatose Brenda, as he slid her wedding ring back onto her finger.

The next morning, while talking to the still-unconscious Brenda, the chaplain touched the wedding ring and Brenda's hand snatched up to her right shoulder. Although she was nonresponsive otherwise, she seemed to display a fear of having the ring removed again. The renewing of vows obviously hadn't gone unnoticed by our mysterious and critically ill co-worker.

As Chuck tearfully recounted this poignant story to us, we concluded that, although Brenda was unconscious, she obviously could hear what was going on around her. Her soul was not sleeping. With this in mind, I leaned toward her ear and quietly urged her to get well and return to our office to clean it up, as she had been promising. Nicole and I smiled, wished her well, and left, still in awe over her concealed illness and the wedding ring story.

The days that followed our visit were also surprising, as Chuck would later share with us.

Two days after our visit, Brenda's harp instructor brought her star pupil into the hospital to join her in playing for Brenda. Too cramped to fit into the tiny room, the doors were left open and the angelic music floated throughout the floor of gravely ill patients. The nurses smiled, and patients were able to relax and enjoy the music. Brenda's response, however, was quite unexpected. She was still in a coma, still physically unresponsive, and yet tears streamed down her cheeks! She could *hear* the music, and she responded with tears.

Brenda's brother, Donald was scheduled to visit the next morning. The nurses expressed doubt that he would see her alive. He was late, so Chuck urged Brenda to "hang in there" until he arrived. Donald and his wife arrived at 2:00 in the afternoon.

"Don is here now, Brenda," Chuck whispered. "You can go now, honey. It's just between you and God now."

Within minutes, Chuck's beloved left her body and, I like to think, floated up into the arms of Jesus. The nurses turned off the machines, and after everyone said their goodbyes, they escorted Brenda's family out of the room.

"I've never seen anyone respond so clearly to what was being said around her," one nurse commented. "And I've never seen anyone go so peacefully."

Whenever Chuck longs for Brenda, he listens to harp music. Knowing how it soothed her in her last days brings him comfort.

The nurses in that small ward learned the value of harp music to their patients, as well. Once in a while, if you visit that remote corner of the hospital, you can hear the faint sounds of angelic music drifting down the halls, bringing peace and comfort to all who hear. And those who hear aren't just those we see.

EXPLORATION

Choosing an Instrument

by Tracie Renee Amirante Padal

"Pick one," he says. I stare at walls lined with pipe dreams
and don't answer. Each slick silver wand and curve of burnished brass
traps my reflection (small hands, odd fingers, missing teeth)
and everything inside me is muted by fear that my words
will come out wrong. He tells me, "Make a choice." I like the clarinet
for its deep, sad sigh, but I don't trust my voice. I point.
He laughs. "Your teeth won't keep the reed in," he says.
I tickle conciliatory piano keys for one summer,
but my hands stumble on every chord.

Two years later, I try again: new school, new teacher.
Same me. This time I like the flute for its shy, lilting trill.
I blow and blow but my lips can't win the right angle;
it won't sing. "This one?" Teacher asks. "You sure?"
I shrug and bite my tongue, eyebrows pricked
to jagged mountains of doubt.
I'm not sure of anything, but everyone else is:
a horn for Michelle, a drum for Richard, a cello for Meg.
A flute for me?

I think about it while boys kick up dust clouds on baseball diamonds.
I think about it under the red-white-and-blue of a July night sky.
I think about it while August heat bleaches soft grass to stiff blades.

A horn for Michelle, a drum for Richard, a cello for Meg, a flute for
Lisa. But I need something that whispers and wails and croons,
even when I can't catch a breath. The lady at the rental store nods
and settles purfled spruce under my chin. I flick the strings.
Twists of taut steel etch a map across my finger beds;
all doubt drowns in a sweeping wheeze of rosin-rubbed bow.
I don't know anything about music. I don't know anything about notes or scales.
I don't know anything beyond the amber-licked flames of the violin's ribs
glinting in the shifting sunlight; and for the first time, I see
not (the smallness of) my hands, not (the odd curves of) my fingers
but the potential in them—

and I say, "This one."

Crushed Beetles and Spider's Crawl

by Lucy Gabriel

I can't read music;
it's a scrawl with leaking pen.
I'm told to think of birds on pylons,
each bird a beat—half, quarter.
I learn by ear.
How long is a beat, anyway?

The music teacher thinks I'm slow,
rather than illiterate.
His hand is a metronome on my shoulder.
I'm told to think of
salt, vinegar, mustard, pepper.
I'm too ashamed to tell him. He never asks.

In the weekly humiliation of flute lessons,
I follow my peers like a puppy learning tricks,
until the week I arrive alone.
Teacher produces a sheet of crushed beetles,
just for me.
I capitulate and quit.

Later I swap Latin for choir,
end up with Latin anyway, in song.
We practice *Te Deum* and *Requiem,*
sing masses, show tunes, pop, and blues.
We perform a cappella at the folk festival,
accompany the organ at Christmas.

Last day of school, I'm called to the stage
still dressed in choir black.
I am awarded full colours in music,
reserved for those who play instruments,
take exams, understand the handwriting of
condiments and spider's crawl.

I can't read music;
I speak it.

Music Looping

by Aleksandr Kuznetcov

From the depths of a musician's brain and onto our ears, ideas are translated into sound.

Heaven

by Bar Scott

Twenty years ago, I was sitting at my piano in Woodstock when I played a phrase that held my attention for the next several hours. This is how songs get started for me. I played my new melody over and over again. The opening chords clashed and resolved, clashed and resolved. My earlier piano melodies had almost always sounded simple. Pretty. This one had some dissonance. I remember feeling like a pianist for the first time. I didn't know I could play so well. This was a real piece of music. Not just something to sing along with. I was mesmerized and couldn't leave the piano. If I did, the magic would end and I'd lose my chance. I stuck with it for the rest of the day, tape recorder nearby to capture my work as it progressed.

I called the song "Heaven" from the start. I don't remember why. I played it for weeks afterwards until I was sure I wouldn't forget the form. I didn't have lyrics, but I had a melody, so I hummed along, singing random words here and there. Singers call this vocalizing. We do it when we warm up, but we also do it if we're songwriters and we're searching for words.

I've learned to trust the sounds I make unconsciously. They often suggest lyrics that teach me something about myself. Like in 1994 when I wrote a song called "I'm Here" for my husband-to-be. When I was working on the lyrics, I vocalized a line that sounded like "my heart cried out." So I asked myself, *what's your heart crying out for?* And the answer was *me*. My heart was crying out for me to pay attention to it. I was thirty-six. I'd always adjusted too much: said yes when I was too insecure to say no; opened my heart too wide when others didn't want my heart to be so open, or they weren't willing to open their own. The final lyric I wrote was "my heart cried out for loving that only I could give." Until I wrote that line I didn't know I was having trouble loving myself, that not loving myself had a lot to do with why earlier relationships hadn't worked.

The piano part for "Heaven" came easily. The lyrics were harder. They took work and an almost complete preoccupation with the song for weeks, if not months, and even then I had no clear sense of what I wanted to say. Finally, I decided to play the piano part at a concert in Philadelphia. I was comfortable there. The audience was full of familiar faces: my husband's family, friends, and people who had heard me sing before.

"I want to play a new song for you," I told them, "but I don't have lyrics yet." Everyone laughed as though this were normal.

"If anything comes to mind while you're listening, let me know. Maybe it'll help me get the lyrics."

The room got quiet when I started. When I played the last chord nearly five minutes later, I held the keys down until the sound disappeared into silence. Sometimes music feels like a place—a location I can go to. That's how "Heaven" felt that night.

After the show my friend Mary came over to tell me she'd imagined children playing when she heard the music.

"They were running around, falling down and enjoying themselves," she said, "but I had the feeling something was about to happen."

I'd imagined children playing too, but when Mary described foreboding, I thought of my childhood friend Dana. Her older sister Susan was killed instantly when a metal bar on a maypole struck her in the head at the playground.

"Sometimes music feels like a place—a location I can go to. That's how 'Heaven' felt that night."

Their mother Vivian watched as it happened. When Dana told me the story when we were twelve years old, it had a big impact on me. I hadn't experienced death yet, but I understood that a mother watching her child die would be devastating. Thinking about their story as I worked on my lyrics, I realized Vivian had lost her innocence the moment Susie fell. She was forced to become a whole new person.

People often ask if I write my music or lyrics first. For me, lyrics always come last. I take as much time as I need, and that can be years. It's hard to say how long it takes because I don't work on songs full-time until a certain point. That certain point comes when a collection of songs is clearly forming into a new album.

I have a small digital recorder that sits by my piano. I record any snippet of music I play that holds my interest. These little ideas aren't anything that anyone else would understand. They're like doodles you might make while you're talking on the phone. Over time I might record ten or twenty short sound files of a song as it develops. When I have enough song ideas, and I think a new album might be in my future, I'll listen to my audio doodles over and over again until the ones I'm most drawn to come into focus. By then, I'm sitting at the piano again trying to figure out what I was playing years earlier when I started the first sketch.

This is harder than it sounds. I don't read or write music well so I don't have written notes to refer to. That means I've got to use my ears to find the music again. Eventually my fingers remember. I often wonder if my ability to reconstruct my songs after so long is because I play the same things over and over again. But the ballerinas that Degas painted come into my thoughts and I say to myself, *it's ok. It's all right to repeat yourself. Some might even call it style.* Telling myself this keeps me from giving up on songs that sound like something I've written before.

After the music is finished—and I mean arranged and recorded by me and other musicians—my need to write the lyrics consumes me. I don't seem to be able to write meaningful words until I hear the music in its final form. Until that point, I may have a word or two, maybe a sense of what the song will be about, but not a lot more. The music gives me an environment to sing in. It's an emotional and physical place for me. I feel it, and I need to describe it in words. When I have a musical space to sing in, I don't think about much else until the song is done. I carry paper and pen wherever I go. This is by far my favorite time of songwriting. It's when I know the song will be finished but I have no idea how.

For me, the music I write is a soundtrack to a movie that began playing in my head the first time I played the melody. Images form, action takes place, and characters come to life. In the case of "Heaven," I imagined children playing on a playground just like my friend Mary did. I wanted to follow them in my mind. The little girls wore black patent leather Mary Janes and cotton dresses with smocking across the chest. They wore little white socks, too, like the ones I wore as a girl. The boys wore brown suede shoes, cotton plaid shirts, and suspenders on their jeans. They played "Ring Around the Rosie." They laughed, ran around, fell down, and got up again.

Later in the song, as my internal movie developed, I saw that one of the girls had grown up. She was lying on her back in the tall grass. A boy was with her but I didn't see him at first. She seemed preoccupied by the movement of the clouds above her, distracted, as though she

"For me, the music I write is a soundtrack to a movie that began playing in my head the first time I played the melody."

wasn't sure it was right to be there. Something had happened that she didn't understand. I didn't either. Then I saw the boy standing nearby, smiling as though he'd won something. That's when I realized what my song was trying to teach me: that one way or another we all loose our innocence eventually. Now I wonder if I was preparing myself.

I finished writing "Heaven" in 1997 before my son Forrest was conceived. I recorded it in 2000. Three weeks later, Forrest was diagnosed with stage IV liver cancer. He was two-years old.

On September 11, 2012, I was asked to sing "Heaven" for the first anniversary of 9/11 at a memorial in Woodstock, New York where we lived. The Playhouse was full. Musicians and clergy sat in a single line across the stage, waiting for their turn to speak or sing. The night air in the open amphitheater was clear and cool. Because Forrest had died six months earlier, and because the song was fairly new, people thought I was singing about him. To this day they think so, and in some ways I am. The lyrics meant one thing when I wrote them, and something else later.

In 2015, my friend Abigail Thomas sold a book she'd written called *A Three Dog Life* to a screenwriter. She was so excited about it that she asked me to submit "Heaven" for consideration for the film's soundtrack. I in turn got so excited that I had the song arranged for a string quintet. A few months later I was in the studio recording it again. The players were arranged in front of microphones in an adjacent room. I could see them through the glass. I listened to their first performance through headphones. As they played their first phrase I began to weep. After twenty years the song had become as beautiful as the film in my head.

"Heaven" Lyrics

Years ago
I remember holding hands
running around and falling down
In circles then, the sun was shining
everywhere
I remember my hand in your hand
And then I find that I remember
holding you in the grass in the meadow
and here I am
I'm on my knees
looking to heaven so far away
searching for my way

In love with you
the sun was shining down on me.
I remember just lying there
the sky was turning like a movie screen
where the clouds roll in fast
and here I am I'm on my knees again
looking for heaven, far, far away,
so far that I can't find my way

When I am here roses are red
a violet's blue when I'm in love with you
When I am here, ashes to ashes
we all fall down and we get up again
we all get up

I'm walking all the way to heaven
Heaven here I come
I'm almost all the way to heaven
Heaven turned away

Why am I here where roses are red and black?
and no violet's blue when I'm in love with you?
Why am I here? Ashes to ashes
we all fall down and we get up again
we all get up

Lydia Rakov performs a dance interpretation of "Heaven" (see the following video; photo courtesy of Bar Scott)

Scan to Watch

or visit
www.sombk.co/v2/73

Listen to "Heaven" by Bar Scott
and watch a dance interpretation
of the song (performed by Lydia
Rakov; video by Jeremy Bronson)

Lyrics, music, and video for "Heaven" used with permission from Bar Scott, Lucy Max Music Publishing, and ASCAP

Voice

by Robert Avery

"Listen," he said, handing down
another stack of records from the top
of the step ladder. "They're yours

to keep." And while I set them
carefully in an old liquor box,
he told me that he used to lie

in the dark of his basement,
and listen, enthralled by the tenors,
imagining himself the next Caruso.

Imagine: my grandfather,
with New York accent and less Italian
than the menu of a stateside trattoria,

who, for all his having suffered
both disdain and fatherhood,
couldn't recount one scene from *Rigoletto*.

When I strained to hear those arias
through the scratches, I could see him
stretched out there after another

taut day at the machinists' shop,
singing on the battered couch,
even into the silence of the final band,

where the solo was his alone,
and the clicks and pops were coughs
and muffled sobs from the house.

Years later, after he'd attended
his first opera, I reminded him of this,
but he cut me off with a laugh,

saying no, he could never do that
for a living, and asked me about work
and the family. For it was not,

as I'd once thought, about some
great ambition for spectacle
and fame, but about a space, free

of cruel bosses and unmindful daughters,
where his voice—normally harsh,
profane when raised—might,

in its swell, be lifted to some grace;
a stage where he might have,
at last, an attentive audience.

Music and Wildlife: A Journey of Change

by Matt Clarke

Music, singing, and acting were my childhood, and I loved every second of it. But the role of music, combined with my love of the natural world, would be the beginning of a very surreal journey for me—a journey of change, extreme loss and pain, joy, passion, and motivation . . . and the most incredible opportunities.

I was lucky enough to be born into a very musical family, with my father as a conductor for the opera, and my mother as a musical show fundraiser. So, as a kid growing up in this environment, I was exposed to a broad range of music from an early age, and I have vivid memories of seeing my father conduct operas such as Wolfgang Amadeus Mozart's *The Magic Flute* in Israel, or Giacomo Puccini's *Turandot* in London.

Music for me, as I was growing up, quickly transformed from an appreciation into an obsession. At age seven, in 2002, I played the role of Doubek in Janacek's *Osud* in a production with the Garsington Opera, which was followed by a successful audition to be a chorister with the world-famous Choir of New College Oxford. From these early days, I knew that music would play a crucial role in my future career and in my life as a whole, in whatever form it would take.

Being a chorister with the New College Choir, I was very lucky to experience the professional life of a musician at an early age, from singing the daily services to touring the globe to give concerts in locations such as the USA, France, Portugal, Spain, Italy, and the Netherlands. My time with the New College Choir was an experience that I will never forget, and its impact on my life continues to be profound to this day. It was during this time that I learned to play the piano, violin, and organ along with my singing, which would prove crucial to my future music writing.

In August 2012, my whole life changed forever. I was seventeen, and my mother, Helen, passed away from ovarian cancer following an intense, five-year battle with the illness.

When we first learned my mother had cancer, it of course had a huge effect on my family and me. I was in school and a chorister at the time, and I still have a very strong memory of singing a solo at a concert with the choir in France, and a close friend of mine in the audience holding up her mobile phone, which was connected to my mum who was in the hospital undergoing chemotherapy.

Throughout my mum's illness, music helped my family and me through our personal and emotional struggles. It certainly triggered new emotions for me, and it gave me strength. In fact, if it were not for music, I am not sure where I would be today.

It was also during this time that my love for wildlife—the natural world and its endless wonders—was also growing rapidly, after watching key figures like Sir David Attenborough, Steve Backshall, Jonathan Scott, and Simon King on TV. As I studied for the GCSE exam, I decided I wanted to take on wildlife photography and filmmaking, and that this was the road in life that I wanted to pursue—to make a career out of it—and with music as a key component.

Immediately after my mother passed away, I began to write music on the piano. Why I suddenly decided to do this, I am still not quite sure. It could have been a type of emotional therapy at first, even though I don't really think of it that way. I was newly motivated with a profound positivity, which seemed to fuel my music writing.

My passion for the natural world and wildlife photography was also a huge help during this time—the natural world was a place where I could go, and the animals would have no view or opinion on what had happened in my life or my personal struggles. It was a world without trouble and pain, which gave me an overwhelming sense of relief.

During my final year at secondary school in 2012, I had written five pieces on the piano, and I was performing them in as many concerts as I could in school, which ranged from school services to ten-minute lunchtime performances

Matt Clarke at the piano (photo courtesy of Matt Clarke)

in the school hall. By then, I was also pushing very hard to pursue a career in wildlife. I was lucky to form a very close friendship with Jonathan and Angie Scott (BBC presenters and wildlife photographers) after having met them at a photography show in October 2011. In the months that followed, I managed to arrange for Jonathan to visit my school in September 2012 to speak about his and Angie's work.

At the time of this writing, I am in my final year at Falmouth University in Cornwall studying for a BA Honors Degree in marine and natural history photography, which I am loving every second of. I have also been very lucky with the opportunity to work as a wildlife photographer in Kenya's Masai Mara, Honduras, and Sri Lanka. And I am now primarily based in Zambia's iconic South Luangwa National Park working for Mfuwe Lodge and The Bushcamp

Company as their photographer and filmmaker in residence, which has been a completely life-changing experience for me!

Over the past couple of years, I have been writing music for my own wildlife photographic slideshows and films, finally merging my two passions. There is no greater feeling for me than combining my love for writing music and my love for wildlife and adventure into my work, and I hope to be doing this for the rest of my life.

Scan to Listen
or visit
www.sombk.co/v2/78

"Retrace"
by Matt Clarke

Mulligan Waltz: A Story of Second Chances

by Sharon Glassman

This is my story of how music found me, and turned me into a songwriting novelist when I moved from Brooklyn, NY to a town folks call "The Brooklyn of Boulder" (Longmont, Colorado). It includes my original song, "Mulligan Waltz," a tribute to the power of second chances that fueled my novel-with-songs, *Blame It On Hoboken* (which puts a joyously nerdy, modern spin on the story of Cupid and Psyche and is set in Frank Sinatra's hometown), and illustrates my personal journey as well.

Scan to Listen

or visit
www.sombk.co/v2/80

"Mulligan Waltz"
(the story and the song)
by Sharon Glassman

Sharon Glassman with her book Blame It on Hoboken *(photo courtesy of Sharon Glassman)*

Road Music

by Marc Goldin

The battered Mercedes taxi glides along on a recently paved surface, snaking out from the ancient walled city of Marrakech, which sits uneasily beside a brave new world of five-star hotels along Avenue Mohammed V. Modernity soon dissipates and gives way to harsh scrubland—desert terrain with occasional village strips or an Afriquia gas station. A camel or two wander the distant hills aimlessly while a Berber taxi limps along, sputtering behind. Eight Berber men inside the clapped-out Peugot smile insanely while hanging onto a car door about to drop off. I was on my way to the coastal town of Essaouira for a day trip out of Marrakech, where I was visiting briefly.

***

I was staying in the *Kasbah*, the old city, at Maison Mnabha, a *riad*, at the end of Rue de la Kasbah, and I walked the main road several times to Djemaa el-Fna, the square and marketplace in the *Medina*—the city centre. Inside, market stalls along narrow, claustrophobic lanes buzzed with activity, while out in the main square, music and performance swirled around like a dizzying tent revival meeting. At other spots, I could hear the traditional, sparse trance music of the Gnawa musicians, plucking single-stringed, wooden instruments in repetitive, hypnotic patterns and accompanied by steady drum rhythms.

There were music sellers in some of the inner market stalls, each of them blasting music that made me stop and linger. A more modern, electronic-sounding Moroccan music, some rap and hip hop, and samples of traditional Rai elements blurred into an exciting new world music, still anchored in the old. It was uplifting to be wandering through a world that was so different from my own. But I was no stranger to its music.

A back story might explain. As a child in the late '50s and early '60s, I had been exposed to global music by my father through his record collection and a yearly trip to the University of Chicago Folk Festival that featured, along with American roots music, music from all over the world. This early introduction took hold and embedded in me a world view of music that would continue to carry me into new realms.

Over the years, I found myself in fascinating circumstances in various places. Like a scene from the film, *Zorba the Greek*, dancing to indigenous Greek music blasting from a jukebox in a local outdoor restaurant on the island of Corfu. In Garibaldi Square in Mexico

City on a Saturday night with dozens of Mariachi bands playing their hearts out—looking to be chosen for wedding or party gigs—the trumpets soaring high above the sound stratosphere. One afternoon in an East London hotel, through the window, came energized Punjabi Bhangra sounds from a music store across the street. Just off of a flight, I was sprawled out on the bed half asleep, the music coming to me almost as if in a dream. Later on, I went over to the music shop and found the CD.

This would be a pattern of mine, looking for music, both live and recorded, wherever I was. Getting into Marrakech, I immediately began my search—looking for small cave-like grottos on Rue de la Kasbah or CD sellers in the *souks* (markets) of Djemaa el-Fna. I took my findings back to my room, stashing them away in my suitcase for later. Sometimes, I'd pull them out and look at them again, trying to imagine what the liner-note text in Arabic or French was saying.

***

I set out for the town of Essaouira around 7:00 a.m.; it would be a three-hour drive each way. I hired a car—a taxi really—for this trip. Kamal, the driver, was tall and slender, friendly but quiet. Initially, I tried to communicate with him but he spoke no English, and I spoke no Arabic and just a few words in mangled French.

The first hour or so was fascinating. I couldn't believe where I was. Driving for stretches across desert-like terrain, spying camels in the distance and a small family on one donkey, ambling down the side of the road. I saw a few robed figures walking, as well. If I hadn't looked up to notice the phone or electrical wires, what I was seeing might've been taking place five hundred years ago.

After a while, there wasn't much to see and the ride became monotonous, hypnotic. Kamal popped a CD into the player. It was a Bob Marley compilation. I like Marley well enough

". . . it was great music for a road trip, cruising through wild country to a reggae groove; I was in heaven, looking out the window and soaking it all in."

and acknowledge him as the patron saint of Jamaican reggae, but I tend toward the hard core sounds—street music you might not hear unless you knew where to look. Ultimately, Marley was mainstream: reggae for the masses, for whom the darker and more raw dub and dancehall styles might be a little scary. Still, it was great music for a road trip, cruising through wild country to a reggae groove; I was in heaven, looking out the window and soaking it all in.

Essaouira is a beautiful coastal town on the ocean and, after the heat and hustle of Marrakech, it was a delight to wander through its more relaxed markets and feel the cool, sea air. There was music to be found in some of the market stalls and I came away with a few CDs for later. I did some more wandering and then it was time to catch back up with Kamal outside the city walls for the ride back to Marrakech.

Tired and dusty, but happy, I climbed back into the car and we took off. I sat back and looked out the window. Through a few convoluted words in French, I managed to tell Kamal that everything was cool—that I had a great time in Essaouira, and that I found it to be a beautiful town. He nodded and we drove in silence, with just the sound of the road.

Then he popped in another CD. I heard a skirl of reedy pan pipes in an Arabic mode and then the drums and bass kicked in, followed by a sax and trumpet. It had a funky groove with a soulful, beseeching vocal—a man to his woman—in a song called "Didi." I thought I recognized the voice, Cheb Khaled, a well-known Rai singer.

"I looked out the car window and watched the desert scene unfold down the road while the music wailed."

There was an urgency in the horns and vocals. More tracks played by other singers I didn't know, but I was drawn to them immediately. It was a Rai compilation mix. There was another song by Khaled, a classic I'd heard before: "Aisha," an impassioned song to his muse. I may have heard it before, but it had never sounded like it did at that moment—in a car flying through the desert in Morocco. I looked out the car window and watched the desert scene unfold down the road while the music wailed.

Rai is the soul music of North Africa and dates back to the '30s, originating in the *kasbahs* of Algeria and migrating over to Morocco, right next door. Bubbling up from the Algerian port city of Oran, it was a bawdy music at first—its lyrics, melodies, and song structures rebelling against the more traditional, refined Algerian music, the lyrics thought to be vulgar by some. It was also political and urban, dealing with raw, gritty subjects that appealed to the more inner-city and economically disadvantaged populace.

Through the years, it evolved, merging with various other types of popular music, even rock and punk. There have been attempts to repress or censor the music, but it has continued nonetheless, and it ultimately spread across the rest of North Africa, Morocco, and Tunisia as well as to France, where there are big North African communities.

During that three-hour road trip back to Marrakech, Kamal played the CD a few more times until it blurred with the wild desert terrain we were passing through—the inside of the car merging with the outside until they became one entity, and I became a part of it at that ephemeral moment. I knew that no matter how many times Kamal had heard that CD, there were moments where he was hearing it fresh.

We got back to Marrakech and then into the Kasbah, slowly crawling down Rue de la Kasbah, winding through the continuous and frenetic activity to where I was staying. We arrived at the small lane to Maison Mnabha and Kamal stopped the car and turned off the engine.

We both got out and I tried to thank him for the trip, for the day, and for his music, but it was difficult in my mongrel French. I managed to let him know how much I loved the music and turned away to go. He motioned for me to hang on for a second, and he reached into the car and ejected the CD from the player. He handed it to me. I didn't know what to say; I started babbling but he just nodded to me with a big smile. I really didn't have to say anything; he knew. I shook his hand and walked away. And then I went up to my room, set the CD on a table, and just sat there.

Sometimes the smallest acts are the most important; a gesture can mean everything. I returned to Chicago unable to stop thinking about how the connections we make with people can transcend verbal communication. And trying to go back and recapture that moment is like waking from a dream: the further away you move from it, the more it fades, as much as you try to hold onto it.

Playing the CD at home isn't the same, even loving the music. The closest I've come is when I'm on the road, blasting the music in the car. For brief seconds, I'm back in the Moroccan desert, and I'm almost overcome with a sense of being elsewhere, wrapped in music with a kindred soul. And then it passes on, into the air around me, where it will continue to dwell till I conjure it back again.

AGAINST ALL ODDS

Vivaldi

by Kevin Haworth

In 2000, we moved to Jerusalem. My wife, a rabbinical student, spent her days walking the curved, uphill streets of the city to classes at various yeshivas, learning in Hebrew and in English, piecing together the knowledge she would need to return to America and become a rabbi. The two of us were to be there for six months. We had lucked into a beautiful apartment in the east end of the city, in Abu Tor, what Israelis call a "mixed" neighborhood, where the graffiti on the stone walls switches from Hebrew to Arabic and back again.

The apartment belonged to a Hebrew University professor and his family. They were on sabbatical in the United States, and we had agreed to swap homes. We had many friends studying in Jerusalem at the time, and when they visited us in our scholar's apartment, with a living room and a dining room and a spare bedroom, *and you haven't even seen the upstairs yet*, they looked at us as if we had won a housing lottery. They all lived in cramped student apartments with cold tile floors. They shared bathrooms with too many roommates and rushed to be first in the shower to get a blast of hot water before spending the day studying Talmud. But we were all young and living in Jerusalem; luxury was beside the point.

While my wife studied, I was working on my first book. It was a novel set in Denmark's Jewish community. Since I did not want to say the word "Holocaust," I would tell people, "I'm writing a book about Denmark during the war years." No one in Israel ever needed to ask to which war I was referring.

Some mornings, I walked with a backpack full of books to Café Hillel, a pleasant little coffee shop in the German Colony, which, three years after we left, would be vaporized by a suicide bombing that shook buildings throughout West Jerusalem. Once a week, I played basketball in a low-ceiling gym on a residential street in Baka. But most mornings, I sat at a desk in the apartment's study, with books in Hebrew, German, and Arabic on the nearby shelves and the army radio station set on low volume in the background. From the window, I could see the towering Dormition Abbey, just outside the walls of the Old City; Zion Gate, with its bullet-riddled archway; and in the distance, the rocky Palestinian village of Silwan, known for its tire burnings and angry demonstrations. Each morning, the Hebrew University professor's cat would paw the computer keyboard, meowing for attention. Apparently, I was not the first person to write a book in that space.

I sat at my computer with the Old City of Jerusalem in the distance and tried to imagine

Europe sixty years earlier—the disappeared relatives and buried valuables, the helmeted soldiers on the street corners, the stripping away of citizenship and work and daily life in Denmark and Germany and Norway, and everywhere else, into only this: *Jew*. As it turned out, that world was already in the apartment, waiting for me.

***

Eighty-seven years earlier, in 1913, a boy was born in Salonika, Greece, one of the great outposts of Jewish exile—those venerated Jewish communities that clung to Europe for centuries and flourished in unlikely places like a craggy Greek city, or an Alpine mountainside, or along the banks of a Polish river.

I learned about this boy from a book I found on the shelf of the Jerusalem apartment—I was always browsing the shelves, a way of writing or getting close to writing without actually writing—and from the first pages, I was captured by his description of his capricious, slightly untethered life:

> *Officially, I was born in Salonika on January 4, 1913. The exact date of my birth is, however, not correctly entered in the official records, as all the archives of the Jewish community were lost in a terrible fire in 1917 which destroyed part of the city.*

Despite this uncertain beginning, the boy grew up speaking fluent French and good German, and he excelled at math, though he also

". . . the apartment and the children and the grandchildren, and everything else in this story, only exist because Jacques Stroumsa was also a violinist . . ."

received the strong education in the arts expected of all people of his class and background. His name was Jacques Stroumsa, and as I held his book in my hand, it took a moment to realize that *Stroumsa* was also the name on the door of the apartment in which I was living.

In the book, Stroumsa talked about how, after a time, he became an engineer and married and had a Jewish son, who married and had Jewish children. His son raised those children—Jacques Stroumsa's grandchildren—in the very apartment where I was standing. But the apartment and the children and the grandchildren, and everything else in this story, only exist because Jacques Stroumsa was also a violinist, and because, in 1943, he was conscripted to be the lead violinist in the orchestra of Auschwitz.

***

At the age of four, my son demanded to play the cello. We were living in a college town by then, far from Jerusalem, and it offered many possible role models and sources of inspiration: writers, artists, dancers, math majors who thought in surreal numbers, and biologists who spent their days cataloguing the genes of freshwater fish. But the person who captured his interest was a round female cellist, who would bring her instrument to his preschool and play for the few minutes that the children could quiet their bodies and listen. Afterward, she would let my son—the one who listened the longest—sit on her lap with the cello in front of him. She held his hand as he ran the long, heavy bow across the thick strings, and he felt the massive instrument sing its deep notes against his small chest.

My son asked three times before we agreed to acquire a cello. The first instrument was only a 1/10 cello—to me, it looked like a shoebox

"He played a collection of jigs and reels—a little Jewish boy who sounded as if he had wandered out of an Irish bar band."

with a neck—but it had four good metal strings held in place by an intricately carved bridge, and the whole thing was made of a well-worn wood that had survived dozens of beginners.

In the beginning, he needed a lot of help. The cello is best played in a seated position, with your feet square on the floor, facing forward, and your knees gripping the heavy instrument in front of you so it doesn't wobble or, worse, fall and become a heap of cracked wood and busted strings. But how strong is any four-year-old? Plus, he was too short for most chairs; his tiny feet hovered a few inches over the ground and the cello swayed like a flag in the wind.

For the first couple of years, I had to follow him wherever he went. I carried a small bench that we had found (in its former life, it was a low table that held a plant in our living room), and I would place it ceremoniously in front of his music stand, holding the cello as he sat down and adjusted his posture and his grip on the instrument, and helping to drive the end pin into whatever crack in the floor would keep it secure. Then he would shoo me away, a bother, since whatever my function, it was clear from the beginning that he knew music and I did not.

He played the entire *Suzuki* book. He played a collection of jigs and reels—a little Jewish boy who sounded as if he had wandered out of an Irish bar band. When he ran out of sheet music, he would sit in the corner of the room and listen to whatever notes drifted inside his head, and then he would play those, too.

***

The purpose of the Auschwitz orchestra was pacification. They played dance melodies and romantic songs as people stepped off the trains and onto the ramp at Birkenau. Along with the neatly tended gardens, the signs for the bathrooms, and the wagons painted with the symbol of the Red Cross, they were part of the theater of deception that was enacted in different forms throughout the camps, designed to move the blinking, disoriented Jews in an orderly way toward *selektion*—toward either labor or death.

The orchestra also played up-tempo German marches, reporting early to prepare and tune, as the prisoners who were held aside for labor marched out of the barracks each morning. (Marching in time to the orchestra made it easier for the guards to count them.) They played again in the evening as the prisoners limped back from work detail to be counted again. They played at the executions of prisoners who tried to escape, adding to the horrible ceremony as all the other prisoners watched. The camps were hard on the instruments, as on their owners. In the winter, the musicians played outside with brittle strings under brittle hands; in the summer, they played from 5:00 a.m., as the sun rose and beat down on them in the *appelplatz* (the place where the daily roll calls took place), until people dropped from heatstroke and were counted no more. The trains did not stop running; the orchestra did not stop playing.

Actually, there was not one orchestra, but many. Auschwitz-Birkenau and its numerous satellite labor camps were huge and bulging with guards, local civilian workers, and, of course, thousands upon thousands of prisoners. Each sub-camp had its own orchestra. Groups were formed and re-formed as members died or as the camp system evolved.

Jacques Stroumsa arrived in May 1943, getting off a transport with nearly the entire Jewish population of Salonika. He, his brother, and his two younger sisters were pushed to the left. His father, his mother, and his wife, who was eight months pregnant, were sent to the right, in the direction of the smokestacks.

He was tattooed on his left arm with the number 121097, shaved and deloused, and given

"His talent was discovered almost by accident when a call went through the barracks for musicians."

a striped uniform with a yellow star. "At that moment," he wrote, "we were made into real Birkenau prisoners."

His talent was discovered almost by accident when a call went through the barracks for musicians. He hesitated—the camp was already a place of survival, not art. But other Greek prisoners convinced him his skill might be useful. He was handed a violin and a bow that had come off a recent transport. He played for twenty minutes from memory: Haydn, Bach, part of a sonata. He was named first violinist of the orchestra. Stroumsa described his experience:

> We stood in the cold at the morning roll-call for one or two hours or longer, our teeth chattering in the drizzle. At the whistle, we began to play as the slave laborers marched past. We played without interruption, for two hours or more.

The orchestras played the same tunes over and over again each day. They played popular European marches and parlor songs: "Old Comrades," "The Florentiner March," "Parade March," and "Darling, I Am Sad." They played two tunes composed by the orchestra members themselves, in the few spare moments they had to write and score, early in the morning before reporting for duty. They titled these "Labor Camp March" and "Work Shall Set You Free."

***

At the age of six, my son played his cello with a folk band in a college bar. Somehow, as the undergraduates drank their beer and racked their pool games and greeted their friends, they seemed not to notice a little cellist, bowing in

"A musician must make do with the conditions."

sharp strokes as the band bundled through the loops of an old-time tune. (I stood in the back and listened. Even with the bar noise, the prancing fiddles, the clack-clack of the pool balls, I could hear him. I can always hear his cello.)

At seven, he jammed with a local musician who is famous for having played at Woodstock. At eight, he played the wedding music for the parents of two of his friends from school. After the rings were exchanged, he put down his cello and ran through the fields with the other second graders and then waited, impatiently, for the cake to be served.

For the first few years, his hands were too small to tune his cello, and mine were too clumsy. Twice, while turning a peg, I snapped his A string: a wicked, animal sound. Both times he cried as if a small portion of the world had ended. The second time, after regaining his composure,

he sat down on his bench and began to play, drawing his bow over the three remaining strings, inventing a tune that required only the available notes. The look on his face said, *a musician must make do with the conditions.*

***

The murder of the Jews was accompanied by a massive criminal enterprise, including but not limited to money, jewelry, rare or notable books, and art holdings representing hundreds of years of collecting. There were at least four official Nazi looting organizations, each with its own hierarchies and geographic territories, or its own areas of expertise: stealing famous paintings, confiscating insurance payments, or looting valuable books from institutional libraries.

Musical instruments were one such focus. Jewish musicians were used or discarded according to the whims of the moment, but their instruments were always valuable. The Nazis developed a task force known as the Sonderstab Musik, made up of German musicologists and classical music lovers who volunteered to identify precious instruments and track down their owners. By one method or another, they stole most of the significant violins in Europe, including a 1709 Stradivari, a 1719 Stradivari, a 1724 Stradivari, and a 1783 Guadagnini. They confiscated a Guarneri from 1742, a year in which Guarneri, one of the greatest violin makers in history, is known to have made only thirteen violins. None of these instruments were ever returned.

92

The instruments were stolen by force or taken from their owners' houses after the residents had been deported to the ghettos. Sometimes musicians were forced at gunpoint to hand their instruments to Nazi authorities. Other times, they were told to bring their instruments into the cattle cars, to resupply the camp orchestras when their instruments broke from cold or overuse. In Prague, home to generations of klezmer musicians, instruments were collected as the ghetto there was liquidated—everything from clarinets, accordions, and pianos to hand-me-down violins, brass marching instruments, and concert-level strings. The Nazis kept precise records: 20,301 instruments from the Prague ghetto were passed to the Germans as the Jews boarded the trains.

There is a story for every instrument, every musician, if only we knew them. After he was fired from the Libau Orchestra, the cellist Lev Aronson was told to surrender his Amati cello, one of only twenty in the world, to the non-Jewish musician who would take his place as first chair. When he asked for a receipt, he was pushed down the stairs. The principal cellist of the Berlin Philharmonic, Hans Bottermund, fled to Copenhagen to protect his Guarneri cello. He wrote a note and put it in his cello case. "I have never known a cello with such a D string," it said. Then the Germans arrived in Denmark, too.

***

During his eighteen months in the camps, Jacques Stroumsa saw his younger sister, Julie, for only a half-hour. They stood next to each other but did not dare to speak lest they draw attention to themselves. Better, always, to go unnoticed. She was also a violinist; she had survived by playing in the women's orchestra in Birkenau. She was

"There is a story for every instrument, every musician, if only we knew them."

small and thin, but her violin kept her from the gas. She died of typhus two weeks before the camps were liberated. "Sorrow has become a permanent state with me," wrote Stroumsa.

***

There are three kinds of memory connected to music, as my son tells me. He is eleven years old and knows many things about music. The first kind of memory is visual; a musician with this ability sees the notes unscroll before his eyes—invisible notes on an invisible music stand—and follows their path to the end. The second is mechanical: through repetition, the hands learn the comforting sequence of playing the correct sounds, like a basketball player drifting to his sweet spot on the court or a dancer feeling the right balance of hard landing and soft turn.

The third is aural. This is the kind he has, he says. "I hear it before it happens," the small boy tells me. "I already know in my head what the notes are supposed to be." It's true; you can

"For him, music is not history but the future, always waiting to meet him."

see it when he practices, his ear cocked upward like an open cup, waiting for the notes to arrive. His eyes are set to the middle distance, seeing and not seeing. The process should be slow, but it is not, not at all. It is unbelievably fast. The notes pour from the open cup of his right ear across the back of his neck and flow up his left arm like water so that, as he plays, his hand flies through the first six positions of the cello faster than you or I can swallow. He hears and sets his metronome faster, faster. The hand charges up and down the cello's neck. For him, music is not history but the future, always waiting to meet him.

***

Among the most celebrated musicians known to have arrived in Auschwitz were the baritone Erhard Wechselmann, the contralto Magda Spiegel, and the cabaret singer Kurt Gerron; the composers Pavel Haas and Viktor Ullmann; and the pianist James Simon, who was last seen sitting on his suitcase before the transport, composing music. None of them survived. Most of the members of the orchestras remain unknown.

***

In the Jerusalem apartment, there is a photograph of Jacques Stroumsa instructing his granddaughter, Dafna, on the violin. Dafna, a pretty teenager, holds the violin while Jacques hovers over her, pointing out fingering and adjusting her bow hold. He seems to believe in the value of technical instruction. I don't know if he thinks this violin may someday save her life. The photograph does not say.

***

I do not know if my son will become a great cellist. His bow hold is unreliable. He lacks patience. His left elbow drops when it should stay high, and his fingers squeeze the instrument's neck rather than caress it. But he has a strong ear and a happy relationship with his instrument. When he finishes his daily practice, he lays down his cello and wanders through our house, humming Vivaldi, Dvořák, Bach. He does not have to play as if his life depends on it.

REFERENCES

Gilber, S., 2005. *Music in the Holocaust: Confronting Life in the Nazi Ghettos and Camps.* Clarendon Press, Oxford.

Hertling, V., 2005. Music and Musicians Persecuted during the Holocaust. *Encyclopedia of Genocide and Crimes against Humanity*, Vol. 2. Thomson Gale, Farmington Hills.

John, E., 2001. Music and Concentration Camps: An Approximation. *Journal of Musicological Research*, 20:4.

Stroumsa, J., 1996. *Violinist in Auschwitz: From Salonica to Jerusalem 1913–1967.* Hartung-Gorre, Konstanz, Germany.

This essay was originally published in Creative Nonfiction *in 2015*

95

Sharing Art Through the Storm

by Kenneth Salzmann

One of the greatest concerts I ever attended never took place at all. Not quite, anyway.

Instead, a violent thunderstorm, which came pretty much out of nowhere one summer night, left the Saratoga Performing Arts Center without electrical power. The unexpected storm hit just minutes before the Philadelphia Orchestra was set to take the stage along with a guest soloist, the violinist Sarah Chang.

Forty-five minutes later, the audience was still waiting, hoping power would be restored and the concert would get under way. That's when Chang stepped onto the stage, alone except for her violin and a couple of stagehands equipped with flashlights to illuminate her and her music.

The orchestra remained backstage. But Chang began playing Fritz Kreisler's "Recitativo and Scherzo-Caprice." Maybe the rain was still pounding on the roof and flooding the lawn. Maybe the thunder hadn't been muted yet by distance. Chances are, though, no one listening that night could tell you there was anything at all in the air except the music.

The performance was brief, but it was delivered with both virtuosic skill and exceptional grace—a sort of "thank you" card for the audience.

The ovation was huge. Then, several thousand music lovers made their way through pooling rainwater and back to their cars.

Maybe the story ends right there. But for me, it has a resonance that reaches beyond the moment. The then-twenty-year-old musician's respect for the people who had come to hear her music also says something about the essential relationship between artist and audience.

Creating art (even if that means performing before a large audience) is in many ways a solitary and intensely personal pursuit. But the moment a creative work touches someone else, it also becomes a shared experience, a sort of collaboration and even, in some sense, a transfer of ownership.

Maybe Sarah Chang understood that when she offered her music as a gift that night, unamplified and in the near-darkness of a summer evening storm.

The Deaf Composer

by Darrell Lindsey

He says he writes the sprawling symphony
from that ringing laughter
beside the bright river
of his youth
before the trauma,
from remembered bells of a church
still sonorous in his hometown
that shape the notes
and marrow of music
now growing on the page
like yellow roses
in his best dream's garden.

He relates in sign language
of birdsong and summer breezes
that once kissed his ears
as gently as the late wife
who still hums to him
measure by measure.

He tells me of the cosmos
so few listen to
as if it were an orchestra,
the way it comes to him
in the middle of the night
through the telescope
of his unblinking heart.

With Just One Hand

by Richard Bauman

When Paul Wittgenstein opened his eyes and saw Russian uniforms, the words "prisoner of war" floated through his mind. Then, with the searing pain in his right arm came an even more disturbing thought: *Will I play the piano again?* The question and the pain drove him back into unconsciousness.

In civilian life, Wittgenstein was a brilliant pianist. Critics had predicted an "admirable" future for him after his debut in Vienna at age twenty-six. But, the next year, in August 1914, serving as an Austrian army officer during World War I, he was shot by a Russian sniper. Captured and taken to a primitive field hospital, the bones in his right arm were splintered so badly by the bullet that the Russian Army surgeon had no choice but to amputate.

Wittgenstein had plenty of time to think while lying in his hospital bed—and plenty of dark thoughts, too. Dreams of his future, fame, and the happiness of music were over—shattered by that bullet. What future could there be for a one-armed piano player. Then, from his depression, sprang determination; this would not be the end of his music. His missing arm would not defeat him.

***

Wittgenstein was born into a wealthy Austrian family on May 11, 1887. He grew up in a mansion full of activity and music. His grandmother's distant cousin was Josef Joachim, a celebrated violinist of that era, and as a youth, Wittgenstein often accompanied him on the piano.

Despite this musical environment, Wittgenstein's father believed music should be one's hobby, not one's profession. Paul nonetheless turned to music, studying piano with Theodor Leschetizky, the teacher of many great pianists. And he learned piano theory from the blind organ virtuoso Josef Labor.

***

Thanks to a prisoner exchange agreement initiated by Pope Benedict XV in 1915, Wittgenstein was sent from a POW camp in Siberia to Sweden. By late December, he was back in Vienna and rehabilitating himself.

He wouldn't let others help him. He had to work it out by himself. "It was like attempting to scale a mountain," he said of those days. "If you can't climb up from one side, you try another." He had to rest more frequently than other pianists do because his left hand tired more quickly.

"Left-hand playing can be strenuous," says Dr. Theodore Edel, a professor of music at the University of Illinois, and an expert on one-handed piano music. "A half-hour of even moderately fast music can bring on fatigue: all the fingers used constantly and sometimes in unfamiliar positions."

Conversely, Wittgenstein said, "It is easier to play with the left hand alone than with the right hand alone. The thumb on the left hand, its strongest finger, is on top. My left thumb does the work of my lost right hand." He also said of his one-hand technique, "I had to learn to apply the half-change of the pedal." He refused a piano firm's offer to install a special pedal for him because he thought people would say the piano was fixed. "By holding the chord with the pedal," he said, "I give the impression of playing the whole chord simultaneously."

Wittgenstein astonished critics when he gave his first one-arm recital toward the end of the war. Suffering had matured him as an artist they said. Unfortunately, for Wittgenstein, there were no concert compositions for the left hand alone. The great composers had never conceived the likelihood of a one-armed pianist playing concerts. Brahms had transcribed Bach's "Chaconne" (from Partita No. 2) for the left hand when Clara Schumann injured her right arm. Max Reger and Saint-Saëns had written a few pieces. That was about all.

Wittgenstein spent months searching through libraries and secondhand music shops for pieces that could be transcribed without change. Among those he arranged and recorded were some of Mendelssohn's *Songs Without Words*, Grieg's "Elegy" from *Lyric Pieces*, Op. 47, and Schumann's "Melancholy" from *Bunte Blätter*, Op. 99. (His transcriptions, exercises, and etudes were later published as *School for the Left Hand*.)

Wittgenstein inspired some great composers to create works that otherwise might never have been written. In 1923, Franz Schmidt, the Austrian composer, dedicated to Wittgenstein his Concertante Variations on a Theme of Beethoven for Piano (left hand) and Orchestra,

"Suddenly, numerous celebrated composers wanted to create works especially for him."

and later his Quintet in G major. Wittgenstein talked to Richard Strauss, the famed composer, and Strauss wrote for him *Parergon zur Sinfonia Domestica*. When Wittgenstein had the audacity to complain it wasn't brilliant enough, Strauss wrote a more difficult piece, *Panathenäenzug*.

Suddenly, numerous celebrated composers wanted to create works especially for him. Some of them were moved by his courage, and all were excited by the challenge of doing something never before done. Sergei Prokofiev, Erich Wolfgang Korngold, Paul Hindemith, and Benjamin Britten all wrote original works for him. Wittgenstein performed throughout Europe to great critical acclaim.

In 1929, Maurice Ravel had just scored a sensational success with his *Boléro*, and after a triumphant American tour he was asked to write a piano concerto for the one-armed pianist. Ravel was immediately interested. He met Wittgenstein in Vienna, and they talked one evening about Wittgenstein's musical challenge. Ravel was so intrigued, he agreed to write the concerto.

Ravel began composing in secret, working simultaneously on another (two-handed) piano concerto. His Piano Concerto for the Left Hand was influenced heavily by the music of George Gershwin, whom he had met during his American tour.

Ravel told a friend about the concerto, saying, "The listener must never feel that more could have been accomplished with two hands. The piano part must be complete, beautiful, and transparent."

Though in declining health, Ravel put much of his energy into it, and finished the work in the summer of 1930. He invited Wittgenstein to hear it.

"Ravel took me to his work room and played the new concerto for me," Wittgenstein said of that evening. He played the solo part with

"The audience sat entranced, and when it was over, they rose as one and cheered wildly."

both hands; and he also played the orchestral score. "He was not an outstanding pianist, and I wasn't overwhelmed by the composition," Wittgenstein recalled. "I suppose Ravel was disappointed, and I was sorry, but I had never learned to pretend." Months later, and only after he had thoroughly studied the concerto, did he realize what a great work it was.

The auditorium of Salle Pleyel in Paris vibrated with excitement the night of January 17, 1933. For the first time, Ravel would conduct his Piano Concerto for the Left Hand, with Wittgenstein at the piano. The two men in evening dress walked on to the stage in front of the musicians of the Orchestre Symphonique: Paul Wittgenstein, the empty right sleeve of his tail coating hanging down; behind him stood Maurice Ravel, frail and nervous. They were greeted with wild applause.

Ravel raised his baton. The haunting theme of the concerto began. "When Wittgenstein began to perform his cadenza, a shudder ran through the audience," Roger Crosti later wrote in *Le Ménestrel*. "He played with authority and feeling . . . it was a miracle—his left hand had become two hands, one singing and the other accompanying . . . his hands touched our hearts."

The audience sat entranced, and when it was over, they rose as one and cheered wildly. They recognized a master composer had written a masterpiece for a master artist. A few weeks later, Wittgenstein performed the concerto in Monte Carlo, and again received a tremendous ovation.

Wittgenstein, his wife, and three children emigrated to the United States in 1938. In addition to giving concerts, he taught piano at Ralph Wolfe Conservatory in New Rochelle, New York, and in his studio in New York City. Among his pupils were several one-armed pianists.

Just after his seventieth birthday, he recorded the Bach-Brahms "Chaconne" and Ravel's Piano Concerto for the Left Hand. Wittgenstein died in 1961. He never retired, and music was always his life's first love. He became uncomfortable when he was away from his piano, even for a day, and spent his summer vacations in a secluded old farmhouse near Zell am See, Austria, where he practiced his music at least four hours a day.

The Piano Concerto for the Left Hand, which Ravel wrote for Wittgenstein, has long become part of musical history. Great pianists everywhere perform it. But it is more than wonderful music—it is also a tribute to the courage and persistence of Paul Wittgenstein.

REFERENCES

Edel, T., 1994. *Piano Music for One Hand*. Indiana University Press, Bloomington.

Oja, C.J., 1998. The Gershwin Circle. American Composers Orchestra, New York. http://www.americancomposers.org/archive/1998-99-season/rel990110-htm/gershwin-htm (accessed June 2000).

The Internet Cello Society, 1999. One Hand Piano History and Repertoire. http://www.cello.org/heaven/disabled/intervie.htm (accessed June 2000).

Wechsberg, J., 1959. His Hand Touched Our Hearts. *Coronet Magazine*, June, pages 25-29. Esquire, New York City.

This story was previously published in Abilities Magazine *in 2002 under the title, "Paul Wittgenstein: His Music Touched Our Hearts"*

I Learned to Play the Piano at Age 91

by Alma H. Bond

As a child I was uninterested in learning to play an instrument, as I was preoccupied with becoming an actress. As an adult, I was busy raising three children and working hard at becoming a psychoanalyst. I may have understood psychoanalytic theory, but I remained a musical ignoramus.

At the age of five, I couldn't carry a tune. When my mother said, "Shut up and let your brother sing," I learned I was musically untalented, and didn't sing for thirty years. I did take piano lessons as a teenager for a few months, from a teacher who seemed to only know how to play with his right hand. I soon got rid of him. Then, when my children were babies, I rocked them to sleep singing, as I figured they were too little to complain.

When my children grew older, I bought a white upright piano decorated with purple polka dots; the piano had a soft, lovely tone. The children started piano lessons. Unsurprisingly, as part of an unmusical family, they "didn't take." I, alone, sat among the polka dots and banged out my old favorites. I was too embarrassed to play around anyone else.

I adored an old book of goodies, the *Fireside Book of Folk Songs*, edited by Margaret Bradford Boni in 1947. To my delight, hours spent trying to locate a copy paid off. It cost $50, in contrast to the $2.98 it originally cost.

I loved writing a biography of the soprano opera singer, Maria Callas: *The Autobiography of Maria Callas, A Novel*. In fact, I loved Maria, and listened to her recordings constantly. My love of her expanded to opera, and I became a yearly member of the Metropolitan Opera. I later rewrote the book as a monologue, and the famous diva, Joy Davidson, starred in my off-Broadway play, and toured with it all over the South.

To my astonishment, at age ninety, I became obsessed with a thousand songs racing through my head. How strange that someone who had no talent or deep interest in music—other than opera—was silently singing all day! Then, in a sane moment, it occurred to me that my need for music is an instinct that was ungratified. My unconscious mind was screaming that I was starved for music.

So I decided to buy a piano.

Not wanting to spend much money, I began investigating pianos on Craigslist and eBay. One man offered to give me a baby grand for nothing but the cost of moving it. It was at least 100 years old. My daughter Janet checked with the company that built it; they said it was a fine piano but would require frequent, extensive (and expensive) repairs. I checked that one off the list. Another piano was affordable and sounded great. But it was in Missouri, and I couldn't imagine buying it unseen. Besides, the price of moving the piano came to more than its cost. So, that one was out, too.

After looking into perhaps a hundred advertised pianos, all of which I rejected because they were too large, expensive, blemished, or screeched like cats howling at night, I found an eBay notice that a walnut spinet made by Estey was on sale for $250, but was worth $800. The Estey Piano Company, according to Wikipedia, has a fine reputation. Although I suspected the piano couldn't be very good at that price, it sounded worth seeing.

I soon learned that every piano, even when made by the same manufacturer in the same year, has its own personality. I desperately hoped the temperament of this piano would jive with mine, as it seemed right for me in every other respect. Its home was nearby, so I went to see it and banged out "Ol' Man River." Despite my thumping rendition, I got the feeling that once I learned to play it, the tones of the piano would flow with a bell-like clarity. The piano behaved as if it were made for me. It was small and would fit nicely into my living room beneath a large window; it was made of beautiful, walnut wood with real ivory keys, and was delightful to look at. Its sixty years gave it a soft patina, almost like a mirror. I immediately fell in love with it, and imagined myself up on a concert stage flawlessly playing Beethoven's *Ninth Symphony*. I knew I must have that piano. Thus it is when one falls in love.

Alma H. Bond at her piano (photo courtesy of Alma H. Bond)

So, I bought it and began to look for a piano teacher who would be willing to take on a ninety-one-year-old beginner.

I counted hours for the two days before the piano would be delivered. When it finally arrived, I began plunking out old tunes. I decided to try to learn the left-hand notes myself before beginning lessons. Mistake! Although I had practiced and studied musical flash cards for hours, nothing seemed to penetrate my ninety-one-year-old brain. So, I decided to wait until my lessons began to learn the left-hand notes.

I soon noted that my theory about the cause of the songs sticking in my head seemed correct. The more I "played" the piano, the less frequently the songs played in my mind. Now I merely repeated in my head the tunes I was practicing. One day, the old ditty, "Mother, Mother, Mother Pin a Rose on Me," kept coming to me. To my surprise, I found I could pick it out on the piano without any sheet music. Maybe I *could* develop an ear for music, after all!

I have always loved "Flow Gently, Sweet Afton." Besides that, my driver and all around assistant, whom I dearly love, happens to be named Afton. So, the first weekend I was free, I practiced the piece for hours. When Afton came to work on Monday morning, I took her by the

"Miracle of miracles, I finished the song without any errors. Afton cried. To my surprise, I did, too."

hand and sat her down near the piano. "I want to play you something," I said. So I sat on my beautiful new piano bench ($89 on the Internet), and I played "Flow Gently, Sweet Afton." Miracle of miracles, I finished the song without any errors. Afton cried. To my surprise, I did, too.

I practiced from a children's book, with a six-year-old child pictured on the cover. I'm sure he played better than I. Was I humiliated to play so much worse than a small child? Only a little. But I was determined to accomplish my new ambition, to learn to play the piano well. I had to prove my mother wrong, that I *could* carry

a tune, albeit on the piano. I also believed that learning a whole new field would establish new neural connections in my brain, and might keep me around a bit longer.

Playing the Piano for Pleasure, by Charles Cooke, was helpful. The book insisted that if the pianist makes a mistake, he or she not continue with the piece until the notes are played correctly. He suggested that the player practice correcting the mistake twenty-five (twenty-five!) times before moving on. So, I spent many days on "Jolly Old Saint Nicholas," although it is highly improbable it is the music Cooke had in mind. A few weeks later, I played the song through—correctly with both hands! I think I was as happy as the day my first book was published.

As far as I was concerned, the piano didn't need tuning. But since everybody else shrieked when they played it, I decided I'd better have it done. The tuner came; he saw; he conquered, so that even I—with my tin ear—could hear the difference. To my surprise, after the tuning, I enjoyed my plunking even more. Perhaps I hear more than I think I do.

The teacher, Jen, a lovely young woman, knows enough to encourage my banging away. Jen was delighted to add a woman of ninety-one to her grammar school clientele. During the first lesson, she taught me fingering which helped me place the notes correctly. Soon, I was delighted to play "Are You Sleeping, Brother John" with both hands.

So far I've continued pounding away for a year. Do I imagine it, or have people stopped laughing when I sit down at the piano? I practice at least an hour every day, as my love affair with the piano continues to blossom.

I found out why I need to play the piano. I was playing "Tura Lura Lura," an old Irish folk song one day. When I came to the lyric, "and I'd give the world if she [mother] could sing that song to me this day," I burst into tears. My mother died over fifty years ago. I thought I had finished mourning her. It seems music reaches a part of me nothing else does.

Postscript

Alma is now playing "Ode to Joy." While it is not Beethoven's *Ninth Symphony*, her favorite piece of music, "Ode to Joy" is part of its last movement. Alma is elated about it, and feels that playing along with the rising of voices, to the rafters, is the closest she will ever get to heaven. So far, sad to say, she has not been invited to perform at Carnegie Hall.

This essay was previously published in the Summer 2016 issue of Active Over 50

Lost and Found

by Philip See

I've been a musician most of my life. In late October 2002, before I was to perform at a company Halloween party, I experienced sudden numbness on my left side, and muscular weakness in my left arm and hand. I missed the party. My wife and I spent that night in the hospital where I was tested for circulatory and neurological conditions. The diagnosis was multiple sclerosis (MS).

I shrugged it off at first. I ended up getting three opinions before I accepted it. I could no longer play guitar, drums, or keyboards. I couldn't even do simple things like put on my own socks or trim my fingernails. As distressing as this was, I knew giving up my music was not an option.

I thought about my late dad who, as a boy with severe Cerebral Palsy (CP), wanted to play the piano, in spite of the fact that his hands were permanently clenched. He taught himself to play notes using the first knuckle of each thumb. He kept at it, and the impossible happened. His hands began to open until he eventually had full use of his fingers. He went on to play the organ all over the South and in Seattle, our hometown. (If you do a Google search on CP organist, you will find a video of my dad, Lloyd See, in his sixties playing a stanza from "Beyond the Sunset" on his organ.)

Like my dad, my deep love of music kept me trying to play. After several months of playing dead-sounding chords and notes, a natural process the brain uses to heal itself—called neuroplasticity, or brain plasticity—rerouted my neural pathways, and my strength and musical ability eventually returned.

Thirteen years later, I am helping other neurologically challenged musicians, thanks to Seattle's Multiple Sclerosis Center at Swedish Medical Center, and the generous donations of musical equipment from music stores and individuals. It's a free program called Get Back Your Music, for which I organize one-on-one and group "jam sessions" that focus on reconditioning the participants' affected areas. By being persistent, patients can invoke neuroplasticity to recover their lost skills. Our ultimate goal? To start a band. (If you do a Google search on "Get Back Your Music Phil See," you will find a video about the program from KING TV News in Seattle.)

To this day, I have never medicated for MS. I've treated it with a healthy diet and exercise, and of course, not giving up my music. Music transcends physical limits—whether one plays instruments or listens to them, the brain responds. Neuroplasticity can work for anyone.

I wrote a blues song, "Brain Plasticity," about my experience with neuroplasticity, and that of others I have met through the Get Back Your Music program. The song depicts how music can give us strength to fight neurological disorders, from MS and CP to Parkinson's Disease (PD).

"Brain Plasticity" Lyrics

Went for a walk to see my baby
When I fell down to one knee
My baby thought I was proposing
Doctor said it was disease

Well, I ain't gonna give up walking
I'm gonna do what I please
and as for that disease
I say don't MS with me
I got brain plasticity

I know a drummer, she played for decades
Man, she could sure lay down a groove
But she had to slow down
for she had found
her right leg would barely move

Now, she ain't gonna give up drumming
cause without drums the band ain't got a beat
Now she tells her legs and feet
She said don't MS with me
I got brain plasticity

A guitarist was getting in a little practice
so he could work on his technique

but his fingers could barely play it
'cause the muscles were so weak

But, he ain't gonna quit guitar
Said the picking's gonna come on back to me
and as for this PD
He said don't you mess with me
I got brain plasticity

So don't give up your passions
You've got to do what you please
and tell that traumatic brain injury
You say don't mess with me
We got brain plasticity
It's working for CP
We're talking brain plasticity

Scan to Listen
or visit
www.sombk.co/v2/107

"Brain Plasticity"
by Philip See

TRANSCENDENCE

Happyness at The Institute in Birmingham, England

by Jerin Micheal

Benji Compston of Happyness, a three piece alt-rock band from London, performs at the Institute in Birmingham, where the band supported JAWS on their sold out homecoming show on March 7, 2015.

Listening to Bird

by Bill Cushing

Flying through scales
he did the impossible, stretching

staccato sounds,
stopping only to change direction.

He found places
in his search for every note

not imagined:
leaving chromatic gravity,

breaking confines,
shooting up into infinity;

then he rested,
hanging on a single, random chord,

bending branches
of music (but never breaking them),

lingering
wherever he chose, staying

just long enough
to make it his territory

and his alone.

The Night That John Coltrane Played Seattle and Pushed Afro-Futurism Forward

by Stephen Griggs

In 1965, America was at a turning point. The Beatles played their first stadium concert, Bob Dylan went electric, Malcolm X was assassinated, Martin Luther King, Jr. marched to Selma, NASA launched probes to the moon and Mars, and men first walked in space. In Seattle, the Space Needle had been pointing to the heavens for four years. And on September 30, saxophonist John Coltrane and his ensemble would weave together all these threads at a 225-seat jazz club on the corner of First Avenue and Cherry Street and make history.

The venue was named the Penthouse, though it was on the ground floor of a ramshackle hotel. Owner Charlie Puzzo, a bartender with a penchant for the promiscuous, liked to name his clubs after nudie magazines. His other bar was called the Playboy.

Puzzo usually booked his favored mainstream jazz artists, like stately but nimble-fingered pianist Oscar Peterson or bossa nova cool saxophonist Stan Getz. But this booking was different. By the time Coltrane arrived in Seattle for his week-long Penthouse residency, he had been catapulted into the mainstream with a sound that led *Downbeat* to name him Jazzman of the Year with the Record of the Year, *A Love Supreme*. But Coltrane wasn't settling. At the peak of his popularity and having just celebrated his thirty-ninth birthday on September 23, Coltrane was veering his band away from that sound, on a mission to ascend levels of consciousness through music.

The night of Monday, September 27 started like any other. At the club's threshold, a sharply suited Puzzo charismatically ushered elegant audiences over carpeted floors to tables and booths, packing them as densely as possible. The club served beer and wine from a bar at the back, and the long, red-brick side walls were dramatically lit in circles of brightness. The ceiling above the elevated stage was covered in mirrored tile so the audience could both look up at the musicians onstage and down on them from above.

At the ebony grand piano perched McCoy Tyner. A prolific composer and arranger, his percussive chords of perfect fourths and fifths defied traditional major and minor modes, allowing his improvised harmonic movement to shift in and out of the expected. At the drums sat the regal Elvin Jones with a toothy grin. His four limbs magically manifested an ensemble of Latin percussionists. Jones' swing was so deep that even atomic clocks slowed down or sped up to get into the groove laid down by his size 13EEE feet. He was not subservient to any soloist, but would lift every musical idea with punctuation and propulsion.

Embracing the upright bass was little Jimmy Garrison, whose sound was anything but. He plucked and strummed at the low end of the strings, always colluding, never colliding, with the bottom notes of Coltrane's tenor saxophone. Caressing a second upright onstage was Donald Garrett. His bow skills contributed long high notes complementing Garrison's low short ones. He also played clarinet and kalimba. Beside Coltrane stood Pharoah Sanders, also with a tenor saxophone hanging from his neck. A wizard of sound effects, he could purr like a cat or screech like nails on a chalkboard.

In the audience was an old friend of Coltrane's, saxophonist Joe Brazil. They had met a decade earlier, when Brazil had a house in Detroit and Coltrane came through with trumpeter Miles Davis. Coltrane attended some of the many late-night jam sessions in Brazil's basement and practiced there during the day. Brazil moved to Seattle in 1961 for a job at Boeing. By the time Coltrane visited Seattle, his first and only visit as a leader, Brazil was working as a computer programmer in the Applied Physics Laboratory at the University of Washington. While the rest of the band stayed at a downtown hotel that week, Coltrane moved in with Brazil to work on music and hang out.

It was Brazil who, during Coltrane's visit, drove the band to the Lynnwood studio of country-and-western drummer Jan Kurtis Skugstad. Coltrane arrived there in search of new sounds that went beyond *A Love Supreme*. He was also beginning to infuse his music with feelings around spiritual beliefs, an approach that went too far out for many fans and critics as rumors of

"Coltrane arrived there in search of new sounds that went beyond A Love Supreme."

LSD use tainted the artistic quality in the ears of many listeners. Coltrane had also been studying Eastern philosophies and practicing yoga, and just a month before entering Skugstad's studio named one of his sons Ravi, after Indian sitar virtuoso Ravi Shankar.

In the studio, those influences emerged as Brazil joined the band on flute. They recorded thirty minutes of music that opened and closed with readings from the Hindu scripture *Bhagavad Gita*—a recording that would later be released on Impulse! Records as *Om*.

The public transformation of John Coltrane had only just begun when patrons settled in for that first Penthouse performance. At a table near the stage that Monday night were Bill Owens, Puzzo's booker, and Ed Baker, a reporter for *The Seattle Times*. In the hushed conversations anticipating the music, Owens whispered to Baker: "This will be like nothing you have ever heard." Baker's review would run in the newspaper two days later. "Coltrane's sound is like nothing else," he would write. "It is wild, furious, dissonant, scornful of conventional rules of harmonics, indifferent about melody."

After patrons were seated and the band began, Puzzo left the club to take in the fights. When he came back from the boxing bouts hours later, the band was onstage, sweating and swinging for the fences.

Puzzo leaned close to the perky ear of one of his bunny-clad waitresses, "They're playing long for a Monday night," he said. "Are they on the third set?"

"They haven't stopped once since you left," she shouted back over a loud drum solo.

The long, continuous performance produced meager receipts, so afterward Puzzo sat Coltrane down and demanded that he take

"Combining Afrocentricity, magical reality, and science fiction, he fanned the flames of Afrofuturism . . ."

two breaks a night. That way the tables could turn over and the waitresses could take more drink orders. Coltrane complied. Most of the time.

One exception was Thursday, September 30. That night, Coltrane followed his muse. Combining Afrocentricity, magical reality, and science fiction, he fanned the flames of Afrofuturism—which were already lit by jazz pianist Sun Ra, and years later would explode with funk bassist George Clinton's *The Mothership Connection*.

Seattle disk jockey Jim Wilke sat near the stage that night, set to broadcast the first thirty minutes on KING-AM. His introduction of the show, broadcast from the club, went out over the airwaves like a countdown to liftoff. Meanwhile, Coltrane had hired Skugstad, who had a studio with portable equipment, to record the evening's performance. With all the club, radio, and studio gear, there were more microphone stands onstage than musicians. Coltrane briefly borrowed Wilke's headphones to check the broadcast sound. Handing them back, he informed the DJ that the song was going to last longer than the half-hour broadcast. Meanwhile, Skugstad kept feeding fresh reels into his recorder, capturing every detail of the performance.

The first set on Thursday clocked in just shy of two hours, with the first number lasting an hour and a half.

According to *The John Coltrane Reference*, a comprehensive chronology and discography, that first song, a Coltrane original named "Cosmos," had never been recorded before and would never be reprised. "Cosmos" includes long sections of ensemble improvisation, a bass duet, a bass solo, a kalimba solo, hand percussion, and even loud vocal groans. Audience applause marks the transition points, but the music never pauses for more than five seconds.

Coltrane's concepts for composition and improvisation were expanding. He had explored similar long ensemble improvisations three months earlier while recording an album titled *Ascension*, which would later be released by

116

Impulse! These recordings may have been test flights for the Seattle performances.

Another concept that Coltrane originated ten months earlier on *A Love Supreme* involved connecting ensemble passages with bass or drum solos. Live, at the Penthouse, Coltrane adapted these solo passages to introduce or segue between songs in his repertoire. So, following the hour-and-a-half "Cosmos," a lengthy bass solo bridged the transition into the full ensemble's otherworldly rendition of the title song from a popular 1945 movie, *Out of This World*.

The unconventional performance of "Out of This World" had a deep impact on at least one listener. Teenage Seattle drummers Gregg Keplinger and Dave Guilland had snuck in to the Penthouse to get a glimpse of Elvin Jones, hiding behind a coat rack near the front door to avoid the bouncer. Three years earlier, Keplinger had been moved to tears by the beauty in Coltrane's first recorded rendition of "Out of This World." The band onstage was still developing the song, but with more energy and abandon. Keplinger

hyperventilated, he later recalled. The slower tempo, wider harmonic backdrop, and freer solo improvisation, he said, was "blowing his brain cells apart."

No commercial recording has ever presented this music, sequenced correctly, in its entirety. Pieces of the September 30, 1965 two-hour set have been sliced up, renamed, and issued by Impulse! in 1971 as *Live in Seattle* and by RLR Records in 2011 as *The Unissued Seattle Broadcast*. The dissection is likely due to its release after Coltrane's untimely death in 1967 and the fact that he created this recording without a producer.

Coltrane would return to planetary themes during his final year on Earth, in his saxophone and drum-set duet recording *Interstellar Space* with the songs "Mars," "Venus," "Jupiter," and "Saturn." It is in Seattle, though, that the journey began. The Penthouse is gone, and so are many of the musicians. But the planet continues to orbit the sun, as it has fifty times since Coltrane's journey.

REFERENCES

Baker, E, 1965. At Penthouse: Coltrane Sounds Like Nobody Else in World of Jazz. *The Seattle Times*, Wednesday, September 29, page 48.

Porter, L.; DeVito, C.; Wild, D.; Fujioka, Y.; & Schmaler, W., 2008. *The John Coltrane Reference*. Routledge, New York.

This story was originally published in **Seattle Weekly News** *in 2015 on the 50th anniversary of the events described in the story*

The History of That Infernal Racket

by Jeff Santosuosso

Les Paul left to live on his own. To Chicago he moved,
worked after hours at the Epiphone factory
until his gadget proved
complete.

He wired his six-string, set up a cottage
industry and got kicked out
for cranking up the wattage
into the streets.

"The log" he called it, 4x4 wood in an empty shell,
mastering feedback and sustain.
It would soon be the death knell
of peace

of mind, that is, for parents in all places.
From now on, mothers and fathers
would beg the guitars and basses
to cease

that infernal racket—the twang, the buzz, the howl.
Rock and roll was on its way
for kids, so fair; for parents, so foul
a sound.

"Rhubarb Red" cranked it up for Gibson—handsomely rewarded,
he has a shrine in the Hall of Fame.
His songs have been recorded
around

the world. The humble electric inventor
inspired grunge, bluesmen, glam boys.
"Red Hot Red" became the mentor
for generations.

Townshend smashed it; Page used a bow;
Jimi set it on fire; Beck used a bottle;
Blackmore filed the frets for fingering to put on a show,
a sensation.

Oldsters could look away, the spectacle they'd avoid
simply by closing their eyes. The racket, however,
the jack-hammering nearly destroyed
their sanity.

Silence *was* golden, acoustic not too bad.
Then axe men went plugged
and tapped, hammered, and bent the strings like mad
with profanity.

Les Paul broke his arm, but not his spirit.
At an angle he had his wing mended.
He played loud so all could hear it
Till the days of acoustic peace ended.
Rock on Lester Polsfuss. Rock on.
Roust the angels in heaven.
Crank that volume to eleven.

Angel Blues

by Maroula Blades

Undress the dark singer of angel blues,
Moan a modal current, molasses sweet.
Reach through the library of sound,
Prospector of ebony smiles
And stay loose my friend.

Visionary of sweet tomorrows,
Hook the notes, do the speak,
You heard long before you dreamt.
Saturate the night with soul.
I'm on your rhythm, sweet, pure thing. Sing.

from Songbirds
by Harry Longstreet

Presented here are three works from Harry Longstreet's collection, *Songbirds*, which captures performances by celebrated vocalists. Pictured left is Bettye LaVette (2015), on page 122 is Dee Dee Bridgewater (2006), and on page 123 is Stacey Kent (2011).

In the Drum's Heartbeat

by Patricia J. Esposito

(On seeing Jason Perez of Beautiful Collision perform "Hold You")

When I lose this body, spirit freed of iron joints,
of arterial sludge and nerves that clench
with the mind's too-critical claims, when

in heaven's ascension, I shake off this tight life,
and my flesh in a puff disappears, I want one joy,
miraculous: to play drums like Jason Perez.

Under his wild halo of hair, sun shining through
that 'fro, I want the fluid rumble of his life's
rhythm, each beat he makes to the singer's call.

I want to speak like him in thumps and thrums,
drumsticks in a crash and splatter, saying I feel
you and you and you, in heartaches and in miracles.

I want to balance on the seat edge, waiting
for the song's next leap, to take it then and care
for it, tap-tap tap-tap amid the feet's pound-pound,

moving us to where we belong, somewhere
in his smile—yes, when I die, I want the agony
of his joy, head thrown back as the last rattle

pours from his arms, a wrist flick to release.

Avett Brothers
by Michael Booty

These images capture an Avett Brothers performance from the end of the catwalk at the Cox Business Center in Tulsa, OK, on June 21, 2014.

GHOSTS

A Message for the Cabbage Head Man

by Darrin DuFord

No flowers—only paint, ink, and paste-ups. That was the style of tribute in front of us. It was early September and cool air was probing the streets of Paris' Left Bank, washing past my wife and me as we explored the wall of graffiti soup on the exterior of 5 Rue de Verneuil, the house of deceased singer-songwriter Serge Gainsbourg.

Inscriptions of favorite lyrics, stencils of the singer posing with a cigarette, freehand drawings exaggerating Gainsbourg's beak of a nose, declarations of eternal love—each overlapped the others, looped around the gated window, hid out on the ceiling of the vestibule. It was far from a rock star's usual, fortress-style abode, insulated from paparazzi and street rabble with multiple layers of gruff security and manicured grass.

Just a few steps from the odd serenity of tiny Rue de Verneuil, the neighborhood's streets were crowded with clubs, grocery stores, art galleries, brasseries, and cafés with sidewalk tables whose chairs angled half-outward in that distinctively Parisian fashion that allows interaction with the street as well as across the table. The pulsing veins of the Left Bank were more suitable than a secluded suburban hideaway for Gainsbourg, who often wrote lyrics about lovers meeting in nightclubs, jazz bands

performing while high as a kite, and visiting love hotels.

Another couple—late twenties, torn jeans, arms clung to each other—had been visiting the wall when we arrived. They were lost in the glow of their romantic moment, but their smiles wilted when they realized they no longer held a monopoly over the wall. I began to wonder if there was some wall-watching etiquette that we'd inadvertently violated.

In this well-kept neighborhood of neoclassical corbels and wrought iron balconies, just two blocks from the Seine River, not everyone has enjoyed the ever-revolving dialog of graffiti. Biographer Sylvie Simmons, in *Serge Gainsbourg: A Fistful of Gitanes*, noted that some residents of the street would whitewash the front of the house, only to find the graffiti growing back the next week.

I began to see the graffiti, forming a kind of crust on the stucco exterior, as a curious, multi-headed creature, a bastard offspring greedily feeding off the memories of someone simultaneously referred to as a songwriting genius, womanizing drunkard, ringleader of the sexual revolution, and France's ugliest rock star. A storyteller, actor, provocateur. All of these personas, whether perceived or actual, had fascinated me, and I hoped a glimpse of his house (or was this a pilgrimage?) would help me sort them out.

***

Gainsbourg's career spanned five decades, with his earliest albums blossoming from the jazzy big band style he encountered while playing piano at Paris clubs in the 1950s. His voice was naturally suited to the scene, the words falling from his mouth in a soothing timbre, like a warlock's spell. He more often spoke than sang, yet his sweet aural delivery often proved deceiving, especially during the song "Du Jazz Dans le Ravin" (Jazz in the Ravine), a narration about two lovers drinking whiskey while driving, finally running off the road into a deep ditch. The couple agonizes in their last moments of life while jazz keeps playing from the radio. The strategically placed drum solo, an otherwise cheerful fill, represents the car tumbling down the slope.

Such an understanding is helpful in recognizing why, in the height of 1960s *yé-yé* pop that ignited the Paris club scene, Gainsbourg offered lyrics that romanticized outlaws (Bonnie and Clyde) and explored feelings of past love rather than celebrating the euphoria of a fresh crush. He nicknamed himself *"L'Homme à Tête de Chou,"* or "The Cabbage Head Man," perhaps drawing power from the contradiction of an unattractive sex symbol.

***

"AUX ARMES," read a red-lettered inscription on the wall, referring to a line from the French national anthem. Gainsbourg re-arranged the anthem on his first reggae album, *Aux Armes et cætera*, which Gainsbourg recorded in Jamaica,

"Several European countries banned the song, a response which, of course, fueled record sales."

and which led to death threats from France's right-wing elements. The block-capital words appeared under a black stencil of Gainsbourg's mug and a cozy Jane Birkin, the British actress, one of his romantic companions and musical collaborators.

Birkin was Gainsbourg's partner in one of his most provocative maneuvers. Ten years before the anthem controversy, the Vatican issued a condemnation of Gainsbourg's "Je T'aime . . . Moi Non Plus" (I love you . . . me neither), a duet that featured Birkin breathing heavily over a church-like organ melody, deemed too hot for the tender ears of Catholics. (On the wall, the song title appeared in a word bubble above a magic-marker illustration of a slender Birkin and a stubble-faced Gainsbourg.) Several European countries banned the song, a response which, of course, fueled record sales. A frustrated Vatican excommunicated the record executive responsible for releasing the single in Italy. But the Church could not excommunicate Gainsbourg, who was Jewish.

The wall outside Serge Gainsbourg's home in Paris (photo courtesy of Darrin DuFord)

On both sides of the Seine, as my wife and I would pass Parisians, each in his or her own bubble of thoughts—a blond-haired college student turned a corner while looking down at her open laptop; a man sunbathed in a Speedo on the concrete riverwalk; a young woman, working in a crepe kiosk, rescued tourists from their guidebook French by switching to a weary English; a couple sitting at a round sidewalk table of a café had a beer during their lunch break, their scooter helmets tucked away on their knees—I wondered how many of them were conceived to a Gainsbourg soundtrack.

How did Gainsbourg attain such popularity? His personality was a cocktail of apparent incongruity—his shyness betrayed vulnerability, but at the same time his calming voice performed mass seductions. He channeled a darker, humorous stratum lurking within his listeners and brought it onto the street, danced with it, made love to it. He even acted out his life as if he were a character in his own songs. After his first heart attack in 1973, Gainsbourg smuggled cartons of Gitanes into his hospital room. But on March 2, 1991, while he was asleep at 5 Rue de Verneuil, the ferocity of a second heart attack did not afford him a chance to smoke off the trauma. His funeral brought Paris to a standstill.

There was something in the silence of the narrow street, with its sidewalks of a width easily covered by a comfortable stride, that sobered my thoughts of the singer. I found myself trying to contain conflicting feelings about him. His genre-twisting and his talk-sung delivery of unabashed provocations changed the way I view

> "He channeled a darker, humorous stratum lurking within his listeners and brought it onto the street, danced with it, made love to it."

the possibilities of music, and the possibilities of what music can achieve. But he was also a hopeless tobacco addict, and was devoted to maintaining the pretentious image of a chain-smoking rock star. The habit destroyed him, along with whatever albums remained inside his *tête de chou*.

Speaking of stardom: Gainsbourg, at times, overplayed the generous liberties of lechery bestowed to such a rarified class of musician. In 1986, he showed up drunk to a live, televised talk show in which a budding Whitney Houston, also a guest, was seated perilously close to Gainsbourg and his hungry stares. I'm still trying to find the art in Gainsbourg's non-sequitur comment of "I want to f*** her" in English. Cue Houston's open mouth of horror. Cue the host's ineffective attempt at downplaying Gainsbourg's English language skills and offering a deliberately incorrect translation ("He says you are great!").

On a more practical front, I have found his lyrics to be a bustling resource of French words not normally encountered in the classroom, like *hanter* (to haunt) and *entrebailler* (to half-open)—something Gainsbourg liked to do to "her Levis." Gainsbourg even succeeded in cudgeling the normally silky French language into sounding percussive in "Le Poinçonneur des Lilas," where his repetition of *"des petits trous, des petits trous"* (little holes, little holes) resembles the trains clacking past the song's protagonist, a ticket puncher of a 1950s Paris metro station.

I noticed that the other couple had already left. "Why don't you write something?" my wife asked—insisted, rather—as we stood alone in front of the wall, which featured plenty of lovers' messages to one other. Alas, I had not arrived prepared for defacing private property,

> "I imagined smoke-damaged rooms inside, where Gainsbourg arranged not just songs, but personas."

and could only find a ballpoint pen with which to fulfill our suddenly resurgent adolescent desires. I inscribed our names, and also wrote "Le Claqueur de Doigts" (the finger snapper) on a small white patch inside someone's puffy tag. "Le Claqueur de Doigts" is the title of one of his earlier jazz numbers with a spy-movie lounginess, one that helped him gain recognition.

There was another reason why I chose to write that particular phrase. The act of snapping one's fingers is an almost involuntary act that occurs when a song grips someone, and Gainsbourg's recordings had gripped me enough to encourage me to pay tribute in front of his house, whether said recordings reflected on a Lolita-esque adventure, pissing, the gloom of shallow attraction without deeper meaning,

or a bored Parisian ticket puncher contemplating punching a hole in his head.

As my fingers brushed against the unknown layers of handwriting and paint, I thought of how many times Gainsbourg and Birkin had wobbled back into that very threshold in a haze of nightclub highballs, ears filled with glassy ringing, until Birkin left him in 1980. I imagined smoke-damaged rooms inside, where Gainsbourg arranged not just songs, but personas. I also thought of how his daughter Charlotte, caretaker of the house, had offered a peek of its rooms to *Vanity Fair* in 2007, pointing to cans of food in the cupboard from 1991, the year he died.

I turned and noticed that the tribute did something un-tribute-like. The door opened. A stocky blur of whiteness emerged, and then froze. No, it was not the ghost of the Cabbage Head Man, appearing in a puff of otherworldly cigarette smoke, answering my message. It was a man with high, defined cheekbones (can't be Serge, then) in a smart, white jacket and white slacks, fulfilling some imperative of Parisian fashion I knew nothing about. He leaned out onto the sidewalk and peeked down the street, coinciding with another man's arrival. I thought I saw others in the leafy courtyard behind him. Charlotte, perhaps?

Fleeting thoughts of opportunity: should I make an inquiry? Perhaps there was some residual energy, some fading signal within the house to help me understand Gainsbourg's complexities. *Excusez-moi,* I thought of asking, *could I just handle the cans of food for a quick minute?*

The white-jacketed host let the man in, briefly looked at my wife and me, and determined we were not intended guests—just fans, just part of the scenery of Rue de Verneuil, just as the wall was part of the scenery. He closed the door as casually as he had opened it. I had decided to stay silent. It was a private house and therefore required respect—respect I offered by acting like just another silent part of Gainsbourg's tribute.

I began to realize that the house would not resolve the tension between the sound of Gainsbourg's songs and the lyrics, between the groundbreaking artist and the chain-smoking letch. I imagined the singer would be pleased with the thought of someone living with the unavoidable reality of conflict, which, in turn, instilled me with another way of understanding his music after all.

And what would Gainsbourg think about the state of his house? The house is a living, breathing home covered by a living, breathing tribute of graffiti. A great way to keep the spirit of Serge alive. The perfect nurturing environment for a ghost.

We began to walk towards nearby Rue Jacob for a glass of red wine at a corner café, the wicker-seated chairs on the sidewalk invitingly facing half-outward. Perhaps they were the same chairs from which a hungover Gainsbourg would sober up with a slurp of caffeine and a cigarette. I imagined his ghost in pursuit, dressed not in some angelic white outfit but in a dark blazer, collar up, top shirt buttons undone, armed with cunningly romantic tendrils. I wrapped my arm protectively around my wife. Just in case. Because the September breezes might make us a little chilly.

REFERENCES

Robinson, L., 2007. The Secret World of Serge Gainsbourg. *Vanity Fair*, November.

Simmons, S., 2002. *Serge Gainsbourg: A Fistful of Gitanes*. Da Capo Press, Boston.

A Hush

by Carolyn T. Johnson

A Hush

falls over the grand salon
as the noisy tourists
move on to the chateau's gallery
leaving me alone to fantasize

as the aristocracy took their seats atop
Aubusson tapestry-clad armchairs and
waited in rapt anticipation for the
air to swell with the sweet serenade of
Pachelbel's Canon in D

the harpist embraced her gold-gilded
harp like a cherished lover
tilted perfectly between her open legs
resting gently on her soft shoulder
its curves caressing her porcelain silhouette
while her slender hands and petit feet
poise over longing strings

her graceful glissandos took flight
into the perfect portamento
crescendos giving way to decrescendos
the melodies teasing and tantalizing
the distinguished senses
of finely coiffed ladies and
gents in silk stockings

but eventually the music quiets
the room stills and memories
hush into my imagination
of refined grandeur of an
elegant departed era

The Grand Salon at the Château de Cheverny (photo courtesy of Carolyn T. Johnson)

Ghost Busker

by William Huhn

There was a summer in the timeless city of Brussels, Belgium, in the mid-1990s, when anyone who had ears would have heard my fiddle playing. Let's leave out the exact year, since back then I placed little importance on years. While I could usually figure out the day of the week, I almost never looked at a calendar and didn't have any set travel itinerary to follow. The circumstance of my being in the seat of NATO as opposed to another city or country meant little to me. Much more important was the naked fact that I'd escaped into the life of music.

My fiddle sang along walkstreets to the rhythms and flow of the passersby. I went at my tunes like nobody you'd ever heard and could attract a crowd. But of all the nights that summer when you might have spotted me perched on the cobbles, the one that stands out the most wasn't the night I went home with the girl or the night I played my fiddle better than I ever had. It was the night I became haunted.

***

Given the heat that August, I usually performed in the cool of evening, keeping to the walkstreets that begin and end on La Grand-Place, one of the great squares of Europe. I wanted to get in as much summer playing as possible. Before the fall and winter weather set in, I intended to take my trade down into Italy, keeping just ahead of the cold, till I reached the toe of the boot. From there I'd make my way southeastward by water toward the Greek Islands and beyond. If I saw the States again at all, I expected to feel like an unrecognized visitor to a land where I no longer fit in.

Although I'd only been at the rambling life some six weeks, conformity and convention had already become like forgotten friends I'd never liked anyway. If all came off as unplanned, I'd follow my music to wherever it took me. If it didn't, I'd remain confident in my talent. And if I didn't make enough coin to survive, I'd lay my fiddle down and die. To live the heart-flame of song, you have to be ready to die for music.

At that point in the season, quite enough francs had landed in my case to keep me afloat. But I had to be careful not to miss my friends back at home and my parents and siblings too much. Or America itself. Any impulse to return had to be ignored like an irreverent child until it stopped acting up. The child might also be lulled to sleep by music or, in the extreme case, smothered quiet through sheer will. Artists can be cold people if need be. When you live for music alone, you can't indulge in nostalgia or sentimentality except for what you channel into your song.

I could have used a friend, in other words, though I doubt this deficit had anything to do with the haunting I experienced. The fun I was having made up for my lack of close companionship. I reveled in the idea that I had no contacts in Brussels. I'd had hopes for Astrid, my standoffish landlady, but she wouldn't have been a contact even if she wasn't summering in France. She didn't like me, nor I her. And I didn't know I was lonely any more than I knew people could become haunted, like castles or old fountains. Had some crystal-gazer told me they could, I wouldn't have believed him; and if he'd said it would happen to me, and on a specific night, I'd have inwardly scoffed at his prophecy. Astrid had a bad feeling about me when we met, but that's because she was a poor judge of character. The woman would have had second thoughts about subletting to anyone, I imagine, but I couldn't imagine why she wouldn't trust me with her living space and its meager furnishings.

Another contact I didn't have was my next-door neighbor. I'll call her Madame Bouet, her real name, since she's certainly dead by now. She was my landlady by default. My rent money went through Astrid before it got to Madame Bouet, but Madame owned the building. The ninety-six-year-old, who stood four-foot-nine leaning on her cane, was all but deaf; and if she understood it at all, I gathered she didn't cotton to Astrid's and my subletting arrangement. So she didn't like me either. And since she spoke almost no English and could barely hear the American

"...I didn't know I was lonely any more than I knew people could become haunted..."

French I yelled at her, try as I might, I couldn't charm her into letting go of her suspicions about me and my Bohemian lifestyle.

To get to the stairway that led out of the building, I had to walk past her door, which she liked to leave open, although she usually sat out of sight. My comings and goings interested her as they would an old gnarled bridge troll whom you never see and you're not sure is actually there.

The night of my haunting, I slipped out just before sundown, undetected. Upon arriving on the square, I listened around for a good player or two to befriend. When suspecting that talent lay behind a waft of melody I heard coming from somewhere, I'd follow the sound to its source like an animal after living blood. I could smell good song. On that night, I didn't hear a single note in the area.

While a little surprised at the quiet, I was untroubled by it. I liked to play solo, mainly. Most musicians or groups around and about La Grand-Place exhibited only varying degrees of mediocrity. Sometimes, those acts or performers would approach me, thinking a fiddle would spice up their repertoire. They saw me as a means of making extra lucre. I was fine on my own, thank you. It was a Saturday night, and I was sure to do well, if earnings be the measure.

The United Nations was hosting a celebration of itself on the square that night. I forget the specific event in UN history that the organization was observing, if I ever knew, but some of us street players must have felt crowded out by it. No one had laid claim to my favorite walkstreet, Rue Chair et Pain.

Not quite out of earshot of the gathering UN festivities, but far enough, I set my case down on the stone and popped the latches. Upon lifting my old violin out by the neck, I flicked my fingers across the strings while admiring its eloquence. The finish was neither brassy,

". . . an unsettling feeling stole over me, crimping the soft pour of my notes."

red-toned, nor burnished—like that of your contemporary fiddles—but a dimly glossed nut-brown, a hue that seemed to enhance the sound of the instrument. It had once belonged to my teacher of twelve years, Miss Gross, the woman who taught me all she could about classical violin, if not so much about fiddle. No matter how unhinged a street jam turned, my playing was (*c'est dommage*) solidly grounded in the formal technique Miss Gross ingrained down in my heartwood.

I slipped the bow from the felt brackets in the lid. While I rosined up, some stray snatches of the UN's opener, a march, got into my ears like the hum of a gnat. Faint applause, momentous speeches, and more stately UN music would filter my way as the night wore on. Now and then I'd also catch the odd crackle from the PA

or a shriek of feedback, sometimes so loud I'd hear it through my fiddling, and once, some wise-guy UN enthusiast tried to shout me down as he skirted by, something about my lacking respect. But up until that point, the night was unremarkable. Nothing unearthly seemed to be on the horizon as I prepared to play.

My fingers fit lovingly around the fingerboard and neck, and I warmed up with a slow sweetlet, "While Roving On Last Winter's Night." All went beautifully. Midway through the song, however, an unsettling feeling stole over me, crimping the soft pour of my notes. I wouldn't have blamed the unrest of the dead for my suddenly heightened awareness. It felt more like one of my ex-girlfriends or someone else who had returned in spirit and was standing in judgment of me. None of my exes had died or fled to Europe as far as I knew, but whoever she was seemed intent on following my melody, and she stayed until the wistful open D that ended the song. Then it was as if no one had been there at all, except for the few passersby who had stopped to listen. And when I started up again—with a set of fast, full-on tunes—I felt as alone as before.

I tossed off "Yellow Gals" and "New-Rigged Ship" without event, but partway through the next one, which I both sang and fiddled, a washtub-bass player joined my small audience at the rear. I'd really been pulling out the stops on my tune, and I wanted to keep going; but I also wanted to get the story on the bassist, so I let my fiddle hang. Himself a rather tubby guy, he came over and asked if he and his friend could "hook up" with me. By his friend I thought he must have meant his upside-down washtub—with its broomstick post and thick mono-string—but he meant the tall guitarist coming down the walkstreet, his instrument at his side.

I was flexing my fingers to work out the knots when the lankier of the two friends stepped up, thrusting his big hand at me. "Fucking A, dude! We ain't played with a fiddler since Munich! How goes it, governor? I'm Tyler."

A spirited shake.

"I'm Bill," I said. "Great."

I meant that. I didn't always, but that night I did. I felt in good form as a performer. Other times I felt off my game, tone-deaf, and cut off from my audience, as if I knew the world going by hated me. It could get bad out there. At times, even, a kind of scream unlocked its night on me while I was standing on the cobbles. It wasn't a sound the onlookers listening to my music would have heard. I didn't hear it either, exactly; but sometimes another type of ghost—the ghost of all that I'd been running from or wanting to keep buried, and all that I'd been trying to kill—smiled, and it came out sounding like a rumor of my death, or something else of a violence I could feel.

That night, though, my spirits had been steadily climbing. The mischief at hand wasn't connected to any of the unheard scream nonsense.

While considering the musicians who'd joined my company, I turned the nut of my bow a quarter turn, tightening the horse hair, which tended to loosen up on warm summer nights. Generally, I gave extra-wide berth to the American musicians I met, not because they weren't any

"At times, even, a kind of scream unlocked its night on me while I was standing on the cobbles."

good, nor because most performed strictly rock or folk-rock—types of music I loved but rarely felt eager to play. But because I spurned the familiar. Somehow, though, these two didn't strike me as the roaming clichés I normally butted up against out there. The bassist put his daypack down against the building at my back.

"We'll let you go solo if you want," Tyler said, his voice a lusty song-ravaged whisper. "But how about doing just one with us? And afterwards you can tell us to fuck off. Holy Christ, you sure know how to get a crowd going . . ."

"Away," I noted.

"That last one, the Irish tune. Ed called it clear across the square! Was it 'Old Maggie'? That's what they call it back in Pittsburgh, PA, steel-country, where I grew up. I hit on another version a while ago in Sweden. Sweden! You believe that shit? You probably know it as 'Sleeping Moggy,' what most people call it. Where you from, my brother?"

I knew it as "Sleepy Maggie."

"Upstate New York." I was thinking of Poughkeepsie, home of Vassar, my alma mater. While in fact born in Bryn Mawr, Pennsylvania, and raised a few towns over, I wasn't in the mood to hear the guy go on as if we were old compadres.

Looking around, seeing almost no one was left anyway, I agreed to let them stay. "It's always nicer playing with people," I said.

141

That was true only if they were good, and by the guitarist's vigor and vulgarity, I could tell he was. As for the washtub player, he'd add novelty to our act, give us a pulse and a prop. It wouldn't much matter if he played in tune. It's hard to go off message even with a sloppy washtub bassist.

"We're all on the same page then," said the washtub.

"Ed, is it?" I asked him, while wondering, *which got there first, the bad skin or the body fat?* I couldn't help it. For a beat I worried about the unhealthiness of his roaming musician life.

"My friends call me 'Tippecanoe.'"

"My friends call me Bill."

"Actually, it *is* Ed. 'Tippecanoe and Tyler Too' is what I call our duo, but that's because I did a lotta X in the late '80s." He pointed to his forehead, then to Tyler. "This one don't like the name."

"How do you do, Tippee?" I said.

Limp as a dead kitten—Ed's handshake.

"My buddy talks a lotta bizarro crap, Bill. That's why we get along! I've no idea why he thinks I don't like his stupid name for us."

"'Cause you never call us it, not even in the friggin' bistros!"

Only twenty-seven, as I soon found out, Tippee Canoe had already lost half his hair. Unsmiling and squat, he stood with his washtub braced under his boot-sole, ready to throb. The guitarist, with his overfriendliness and lengthy dirty-blonde hair, looked like the younger of the two. I struggled to get my mind around his advanced years: thirty-six. Their ages could have been reversed.

"What do you want to do?" Tyler asked me, looking up from where he'd stooped to open his case, pull off a silken cover, and gently take out his acoustic: a pristine Martin. Tyler got his clothes from thrift shops but sure as heck hadn't skimped on his guitar.

"How about 'Fire on the Mountain'?"

A good musician cares for his instrument as a soldier for his rifle. That's another thing Miss Gross taught me, knowing the warrior symbolism would stick. Standing, Tyler ran the guitar strap over his shoulder and connected it to the brass button where the neck met the body. He handled his instrument with reverence, adding to my suspicion of talent.

As for my instrument, it didn't belong in those streets. It was made by a famous old German family and worth far more than Tyler's Martin. Miss Gross hadn't known the value of the violin she'd sold me, not long before my last lesson, or maybe she did. In any case, I was glad to have a memento of her when she died some years later, of disease linked to drink and smoking, but I had to go to Europe to grasp her real legacy. If I focused my playing on "mere"—as she would have it—folk tunes, just by being out there I proved that her life's passion had caught in the heart of another. She never learned that I too had come to feel the calling.

We jumped straightaway into "Fire on the Mountain." My hunch panned out: Tyler delivered on his axe, while simultaneously singing, belting, and baiting the audience, a born showman. I crooned and fiddled. Ed plucked the chord of his washtub about as good as any gimcrack bassist I'd known, but he also had a funky way of giving a grunt here and there. Our first song left me hungry for another.

Tyler cracked the seal on a fifth of Brennan's Irish Whiskey he'd taken from Ed's daypack and, after a pull, wiggled it in the air. "Anyone?" Ed took it first, then I. And with that we struck up a medley of bright modal tunes. Ed kicked up the tempo when he needed to, and Tyler broke into yodels. We began to mesh and congeal as a trio.

By the time we lit on our next offering, the high lonesome sound of a straight bluegrass set, you wouldn't have known we'd never played together before. Everyone who'd left seemed to have come back with ready claps. Between songs, while we thought on what to play next, the whiskey circulated. People howled and stomped. The coins and bills were pouring in as fast as new faces appeared in the narrows we filled with night music, our sound echoing off the banks of windowed granite cresting over us.

"Let's ratchet this up a notch," I said. "How's that bottle doin'?"

"No harm in imbibing on the job a little," Ed declared, "seeing this ain't a permanent position. *Sláinte!*" He drank, scowled, and pushed the whiskey my way.

Just before drinking, I asked, "How long you been a busker?" I had just learned this word—from *buscar*, "to search" in Spanish.

"Me?" Tyler said. "I don't know. Like, fifteen years. You?"

"Oh, about a few weeks."

"I been doing this shit too long's all I know." The tips of Ed's digits were wrapped with bandage tape so the string wouldn't cut into them when he plucked. "In fact, as of right now, it's a thousand and one nights to the night. *Sláinte!*" He tilted in another all-loving swallow, grimaced fiercely, and held the bottle at arm's length for someone to take away from him.

I volunteered. I was having too much fun, and had already had too much to show restraint.

"The only word on the street was that you had to hear this runaway fiddler."

I'd forgotten all about the scream that no one hears. No rumors that I was lost or astray, or even on my way down, were flying, as far as I knew. The only word on the street was that you had to hear this runaway fiddler. I still hadn't seen any actual signs of the presence I'd sensed earlier (not that I'd have recognized them if I had). And I genuinely liked these musicians. Clearly they'd brought nothing ominous, but rather, only goodness to the party. Death hides in confined spaces, even inside acoustic instruments no doubt, but I'd have felt it had anything along that line been inside theirs. There are a lot of things you don't feel, but the presence of the dead returned is not one of them.

The feeling that I was being watched arose again, however—with much more intensity—during our next number. Of course, I *was* being watched, by about twenty people by then, but the gaze came from other quarters. Looking back, I suspect it was on me throughout the whole song;

but as in the first instance, it was only toward the last measures that I felt it. We were playing the ditty "One Meatball," our most outlandish offering of the night up until that point. This respectable Civil-War-era ballad became, in our paws, a bawdy comic sing-along, which I sang and fiddled like a perfect degenerate, though well. I availed myself of a rabid rubato style, tossing my classical training to the proverbial dogs. My bow was a screecher, and I brazenly veered off key into flat and sharp notes, mostly by design.

Having broken free and far afield of the song's rightful frame, we weren't sure how to end the thing. I'd shifted in close to elfin Ed, who was thrumming away on his tub. About six inches

"I became aware, as of a dream remembered, that the visitant had tried to speak to me."

shorter than I, he reminded me of a tot awaiting his spoonful of mush, his eyes fixed on mine. Tyler was also watching me, also looking for my signal to "take it out." Then I felt another pair of eyes on me. I raised my shoulders and arms high and nodded once, then twice. . . . I didn't hear anything strange, except our music, but the look weighed heavy on me. On my third nod, I dropped my shoulders and chin; my bow slid off the strings, and our roadside combo sank into a zone of sheer stillness.

A kind of surreal quiet ensued. For a breath, no hoots or cheers issued from our score of listeners. Then the clapping began, a sound like frozen snow or ice sloughing off branches in the woods when the wind blows through. I scanned the faces, vacantly looking for the old girlfriend. Then I became aware, as of a dream remembered, that the visitant had tried to speak to me. The words were fainter than audio bleed coming from the other side of a tape—or from the other side of time and the years themselves. The voice had sounded on a bandwidth my eardrums couldn't pick up. The presence as felt did little else to reveal itself, but seemed to know me and just where to find me.

"You are one sick dude!" Tyler told me; "I fucking love you." After bear-hugging me, he went down to his case to dig in its "pick compartment" for a string to replace the one he'd snapped by strumming with too much heart. I called for the bottle, hit on it deep, then let Ed put it back in his pack. Tyler attached a cranking tool to his guitar peg to facilitate the quick unspooling of the broken string. Blood on one of his knuckles marked where the strands of steel had chafed it raw during the interludes he played like pure spirit.

Tyler rose up plucking his new string. I thought I heard German gurgling through a distant loudspeaker on La Grand-Place and considered abandoning our gig to go see what was going on. Instead, I flexed my fingers some more, checked my inhibitions at the starting gate, and with flying "potatoes" launched another set of breakneck tunes.

Our trio's fans continued to accumulate. Rue Chair et Pain grew congested as they piled in wall to wall. Half had come just to see what all the to-do was about, not actually to listen to us. You couldn't hear much of anything anyway over the squeals, hollers, and showers of applause. And during our violent rendering of the ballad "I Know You Rider," a drunken stampede of students—a fraternity of some unknown order—poured down our walkstreet and plowed straight into us, shouting their own song. They strove to out-sing us, to banish the spirit of our byway *fête* and replace it with theirs. We tried to compensate by grinding our music louder, madder, and as fast as our fingers could handle.

When we came around to the chorus again, the forty or so people in our faction were screaming, "I know you rider gonna miss me when I'm gone! I know you rider gonna miss me when I'm gone!" Most of the lyrics of the fraternity's song, in viscid French, eluded me. I couldn't hear my own bow strokes. And I was so rocked that if the dead returned during that interval, I wouldn't have known. If I couldn't hear Ed's washtub, Tyler's git, the boys, nor even my own fiddle, I certainly couldn't have heard the scream that no one hears nor a passerby speaking on a frequency outside the faculty of human hearing.

The night's din peaked during that riot contest and subsided as the last of the onslaught marched through us. I signaled Tyler and Ed, nodding once, twice, thrice. . . . The crowd was just in pieces. And before the whistles and plaudits died down, someone called out asking for our name.

Nobody heard Ed say, "Tippecanoe and Tyler Too," because he didn't say it. Rather, he

"... I was so rocked that if the dead returned during that interval, I wouldn't have known."

yawned with drunkenness, while at once the years of unfettered living caught up with Tyler. The two of them took a break. I answered a request to play *"quelque chose de classique"* by digging out a Dvořák piece I remembered from my childhood lessons. I paid close attention to the formal technique I'd been known to butcher. On that one at least, I did old Miss Gross proud.

After we settled on our next tune, Tyler announced—without warning—that it would be our last. "Ducks on the Pond" felt over before it began. By the end, just three onlookers remained; and everyone who'd left wandered off without dropping a franc. After divvying up the pot, despite the splash we'd made, we each came away with the paltry equivalent of about twenty US dollars. I didn't know Astrid's apartment phone number, but Tyler wrote down the number of "a girlfriend in Dublin"—the least impossible means of contacting him. The guy seemed to live everywhere. Then he and Ed struck out for the van they traveled in, and I never saw them again.

***

The terraces along the perimeter of the square were lively with people speaking French, Flemish, German, English, and Japanese. Everybody was smoking. The scaffold fronted by

145

the blue and white UN banner stood lifeless and untenanted. I walked on.

The farther I got from the blaze of La Grand-Place, with everyone behind walls by then and the cars all parked, the quieter the streets. A ratty dog vanished quickly into an alleyway when it saw me. I liked being in those back streets late at night, but that night I felt lost; not lost as would mean not knowing where I was—I knew where—but in that no one else knew. I'd walked off my alcohol *bien des fois* before along Rue de la Paille. The trouble was, at that point, the closer I got to Madame Bouet's building, the more lost I became.

I climbed the stairs. On entering the dark, stuffy apartment, I immediately regained my bearings. I switched on the ceiling light, its fan blades unturning, and for the first time since

"Then the voice was urging me to hold my violin up 'nice and tall' . . ."

living there, I picked up the receiver, thinking I'd splurge on a call to Kyle Gethin, a close friend Stateside. Astrid had mentioned nothing about phone bills. . . . No wonder: the line was dead. No wonder no one ever called there. At once I recognized the obvious: Astrid herself had only recently moved in. I lived in a place people abandoned before they were ever really there.

I switched the light back off when I heard my next-door neighbor's—Madame Bouet's—door opening. Her broken ears couldn't have detected my homecoming, but she knew I was there. She knew I was by the intuition God gives the elderly. I never escaped her knowing.

At the bank of windows at the end of the room, I quietly opened one and looked out at the streetlamps and treetops and down at the ghostly pathways that sidewalks become at night, the cool air on my face. Bathed in a dimly greenish glow, I lit a Gaulois Bleu. The whiskey, the night, and the novelty of the French cigarettes made for an unworldly effect.

When my landlady's hinges whined again, I tapped off the Bleu ash and kept my gaze out the window, but I was listening. With the lid of her coffin closed for the night, her fleshless fingers worked the locks—first the bolt, then the chain. My dread of solitude came back on me; for what is another's loneliness but our own in disguise? Then something else clicked, a hushed pop as happens in rooms, a door-frame or joist settling. I resisted turning around to look for the woman not there, but I snapped the glowing ember into the night and turned anyway. The felt presence hovered in the room, a thing less than breathing, a spirit both haunting and haunted by me.

While the frequency on which the lady spoke, that of a faraway station, came in clearer at that hour, most people would have heard nothing. I too had trouble lifting her phrases free of the night's white noise, especially with the open window. But the question, "Why don't you listen to yourself when you play?" arose, plus something about my sounding like "a man down a well" when I got lazy. Then the voice was urging me to hold my violin up "nice and tall," not to rest the neck on my wrist. And to be mindful of my technique, always, not just when "trying" Bach or Dvořák. Even the folk stuff I was wasting my talent on deserved at least the poor justice flesh and blood could give it.

I knew that voice. If I'd listened, I could have heard it every time I put my violin to my neck. Before I struck a note, I could feel her adjusting my form. After, I could feel her running commentary. But I was mostly unaware or dismissive of the voice. Even in that moment, for instance, I disputed to myself her doubts about mountain music. But it wasn't the time for discord. She had sought out my violin—her violin—across a continent and years of absence. I could count on her to be listening wherever I went, with her rare ear, even when I fiddled to an audience of none, and even if defying her counsel, if that's what my beautiful folk song demanded of its player.

To pay your proper respects to a lady like Miss Gross, long after having missed her funeral, you'd have to play the tunes better than a boy ever had. I could do little more than thank her softly aloud for her lessons and promise that her spirit came through in every measure.

After this small, prayer-like gesture, the only sound in the room was the call of the music. Like the unheard scream, it too came from a place that few may ever find and, often in the years that followed, a place that no one at all could find, because that's what I sometimes became in the squares and streets: no one. But I answered the call. The grave could have had me for all I cared. The ones who give themselves to music—like Miss Gross, like Tyler and Ed—live beyond this life.

Scan to Listen

or visit
www.sombk.co/v2/147

"I Know You Rider"
by William Huhn
and friends

An earlier version of this story was published in the Jabberwock Review *in Summer 2011*

The Best Seats in the House

by Zachary J. Lee

"She's got the best seats in the house now, I'm
sure of it," they all claimed. I just wanted
to perform. I never worried about
you making it. You always found a way.

I didn't dream of you for two whole months.
I waited, night after long night, digging
my ears into the pillow, waiting for
you to whisper some harmony again.

There were snapshots: disco music when we'd
sweep the house top-down, Adele's *19* full-
blast in the van en route to school, Jason
Mraz fedora-clad at festivals.

There was "Perth" in the car the morning you
let on by mistake that it would come. I
cried so hard and so well my temples throbbed,
music washing over the sodden streets.

There was City and Colour for the whole
first year. I play him still on murky days
when music seems to pass through halls and from
mouths but falls lifeless in front of my face.

There were lullabies, backed up by the whir
and droning of the respirator, Death
Cab for Cutie and Édith Piaf as
I rubbed your back at two, three, four a.m.

"Hearing is the last to go, they say," the
nurse assured my dad in the kitchen. I
wasn't ready. We didn't know how soon.
I wanted a *reprieve*, not a *fine*.

A twenty-first-century breath pushed its
way through clear silicone to the ribbed and
fleshy cartilage of your nose. "Hey, Mom.
Headed to rehearsal. See you later."

You finally caught me somewhere between
here and there, a somnolent recital.
I raced to you in the audience. "I
wish you'd stick with music," you said.
                                        I did.

Memoir

by Michael Lee

Memoir is an ode to lost love. To those spine-tingling connections that happen when you've left all your baggage at home and all that remains is an open heart. After a few intense days, it's back to reality and you're left thinking, *was that person even real?* Our hearts want to chase that love, to hang on to it forever, but all we're left with are those scrapbook memories of life—the pages that we've filled with our love and loss stories. As we flick through, we find a blank page and we're reminded about how this all started in the first place. These blank pages of life are those collected moments of an open heart that go on to form our memoir.

"Memoir" Lyrics

String your cold heart out
Leave it out to dry
Until that old bell sounds
You only wonder why
What good is the garden that doesn't grow
What good is the house that isn't home

Fought a war with myself
Down in London town
Scrapbook memories
They won't bring me down

Face the light you've found
Saying last goodbyes
Feet upon the ground

Scan to Listen
or visit
www.sombk.co/v2/150

"Memoir"
Lyrics by Michael Lee;
music by
David Christopher

As your heart still flies
What good is the garden that doesn't grow
What good is the house that isn't home

Fought a war with myself
Down in London town
Scrapbook memories
They won't bring me down

Take all of my secrets, read from cover to cover
Well you can never be my lover, I'm a man not a moment
So float back to Paris, I'm sure that you're an angel
Alone is where I'll be caught between all the pages of yesterday
Finding shattered dreams
What good is the garden that doesn't grow
What good is the house that isn't home

Won the war with myself
Down in London town
Scrapbook memories
Will never bring me down

What good is the garden that doesn't grow
What good is the house that isn't home
To know where we're going got to know where we've been
Saw your prayers had been answered in broken dreams

High School Band

by Gary Bloom

It's at least three miles
from my home to my old high school
but I can still hear the thumping drums
of the high school band on clear
cool September evenings before
the big game, and the deep
throated tubas and even
the clarinets ride on the currents
of thin Minnesota air
knocking back molecules one against
the other like Newton's Cradle
finally landing on my ear.

Prayer with Conch Shell

by Chinmoy Biswas

This image was taken on a *ghat* (a step) at Varanasi, the holy city of Hinduism in India, where priests are praying to Ganga Devi and blowing Conch Shell, part of a nightly ritual.

About Hungry for Music

Hungry for Music is a non-profit organization that supports music education and cultural enrichment by acquiring and distributing quality musical instruments to underserved children with willing instructors and a hunger to play. At Hungry for Music, their most important service is putting musical instruments into hungry hands. They serve children who demonstrate a desire to learn music as well as teachers who have students willing to learn.

By sharing instruments and musical experiences, Hungry for Music gives children, who would not normally have the opportunity, to experience a kind of freedom and self-discovery that is often stifled in an atmosphere of economic hardship. All of their events, benefits, instrument drives, and CDs are aimed at uplifting those lives and enriching culture at large by spreading the availability of music education.

Hungry for Music, founded by Jeff Campbell, has donated nearly 10,000 instruments in the last twenty-two years and impacted many thousands more children. They have donated musical instruments in forty-eight states and twenty countries in the organization's history. The program is only successful because of its supporters, and as the demand for instruments is increasing, they will need ongoing help to continue bringing the gift of music to those individuals and programs in need. Scan the QR code below to learn more about Hungry for Music and how you can get involved.

How you can get involved

- Purchase CDs and t-shirts at the Hungry for Music Store
- Donate an instrument
- Donate funds directly to Hungry for Music
- Volunteer to transport instruments, hang flyers, or work at events

Scan to Learn More

or visit
www. hungryformusic.org

Read community stories
Donate
Get involved

About Music & Memory

MUSIC & MEMORY^{SM} is a nonprofit organization that brings personalized music into the lives of the elderly or infirm using digital music technology, vastly improving quality of life. They train elder care professionals in nursing homes and other settings, as well as family caregivers, how to create and provide personalized playlists using iPods, enabling those struggling with Alzheimer's, dementia, and other cognitive and physical challenges, to reconnect with the world through music-triggered memories.

By providing access and education, and by creating a network of MUSIC & MEMORY^{SM} Certified Care Organizations, Music & Memory aims to make this form of personalized therapeutic music a standard of health care.

The astonishing results of Music & Memory's program are documented in *Alive Inside*, a film by Michael Rossato-Bennett that follows Music & Memory founder Dan Cohen on his journey to bring music to those in need. This uplifting film chronicles the stories of multiple individuals around the United States and Canada who have experienced the healing power of music through the MUSIC & MEMORY^{SM} Program, including the story of Henry who suffered from dementia for a decade and would barely speak until Music & Memory set up an iPod program at his nursing home. *Alive Inside* was the winner of the 2014 Sundance Film Festival Audience Award for US Documentary. Scan the QR code below to watch Henry's story, order *Alive Inside*, donate, or get involved with Music & Memory.

How you can get involved

- Become a volunteer to help raise awareness
- Host an iPod donation drive
- Give an iPod
- Bring MUSIC & MEMORY^{SM} Certification to your care organization
- Donate funds directly to Music & Memory

Scan to Learn More
or visit
www. musicandmemory.org

Watch Henry's story
Order *Alive Inside*
Donate and get involved

Acknowledgments

Yet again, I have been given the honor to work with a host of talented authors and artists from around the world, each of whom has entrusted me with their work to create another volume of *Stories of Music*. I am incredibly thankful to each contributor for sharing their stories, for walking with me through this journey of compiling an anthology, and for their continued support along the way. It gives me great pride to present all of these works together for readers to experience some of music's many universal gifts.

While putting *Stories of Music*, Volume 2 together, I had immense support from Scott Lorenz, who has been busy promoting the anthology series—so much more than I could have done on my own—and from Kim Retzlaff, who continues to bestow upon me her editing expertise. She has truly made me a better editor.

My husband, R.J. Nashleanas, and my parents, Robert and Wendy Tripp, provided unwavering support and encouragement throughout this project. I extend my gratitude to each of them for helping me further pursue *Stories of Music*.

The folks at Yudu continue to offer a stellar publishing tool, which allows me to create an interactive experience for readers. They have really brought this concept to life, and they've been an amazing partner.

Last but not least, I would like to thank Jeff Campbell at Hungry for Music, and Dan Cohen and Justin Russo at Music and Memory, for collaborating with me on this project. Their work to spread the joy of music is an inspiration to me, and I'm certain they will create many amazing stories about music—and its impact on humankind—for years to come.

- Holly E. Tripp

About the Contributors

(in alphabetical order)

ATA MOHAMMAD ADNAN is a doctor by profession, and a photographer out of passion. He is a street photographer who loves to photograph people around his hometown in Chittagong, Bangladesh, and in all the places he travels with his beloved camera. He has won national and international awards including 1st Place, Bangladesh in the National Awards as part of the 2015 Sony World Photography Awards. Follow Adnan's work at www.facebook.com/aadnansphotography.

ANNA ALFEROVA is a Moscow-based photographer whose work is often inspired by music and has been featured in several local exhibits. She graduated from Moscow State University where she studied the history of photography. Learn more about her work at www.alferovaphotography.com.

ROBERT AVERY is a teacher and musician from Bucks County, Pennsylvania, where he lives with his wife and two sons. His poems have appeared in such journals as *The Southern Review*, *Mid-American Review*, *Brilliant Corners*, and *Verse Daily*.

PRERNA BAKSHI is a writer, poet, and activist of Indian origin, currently based in Macao, China. She is a Pushcart Prize nominee and the author of the recently released, full-length poetry collection, *Burnt Rotis, With Love*, which was long-listed for the 2015 Erbacce-Press Poetry Award in the United Kingdom. Her work has been published widely, most recently in *Red Wedge Magazine*, *Off the Coast*, *Kabul Press*, *TRIVIA: Voices of Feminism* and *Peril Magazine: Asian-Australian Arts & Culture*, as well as anthologized in several collections. Learn more about Bakshi and her work at www.prernabakshi.strikingly.com.

TOMMY BALLEW is an elementary school counselor with Spokane Public Schools. This vocation came about late in life, and was preceded by a patchwork of pursuits which included laborer on the Alaskan pipeline (Prudhoe Bay), a carney, a UPS delivery driver, a bartender/waiter, a long-haul/short-haul dispatcher for a trucking company, horse track racing cameraman, and program director with a fundraising company to support school music programs.

Ballew was the drummer in the musical group 4 Out Of 5 Doctors, hailing out of Northern Virginia. The group released two albums in the early '80s on Nemporer Records: an eponymous debut album and the follow up, *Second Opinion*. The "Doctors" toured extensively across the United States in support of these recorded works and opened for several noteworthy bands of that era, including the Clash, Hall & Oates, the Cars, Cyndi Lauper, Rainbow, Pat Travers, and Jim Carroll (who was also the author of the popular novel *The Basketball Diaries*). The Doctors were reviewed quite favorably by critics and fans alike for both their recorded works, and for their live performances. They achieved modest success, and disbanded in 1984.

Ballew is a husband, a father, and a grandfather. He creates music when it calls to him, and has been seen in the last couple of years performing songs he has written on the mandolin and ukulele for his kindergarten and first-grade students at the two schools he serves.

RICHARD BAUMAN enjoys writing about little known nuggets of history, lesser-known historical sites, and places worth visiting. When he visits places of interest he also photographs them. He's a history sleuth and always on the lookout for photo opportunities. One of his goals is to weave obscure and commonly known information together into captivating stories. He reads a lot, travels a lot, and takes more pictures than he'll ever use. He and his wife, Donna, have been married fifty-five years, have two grown children, four grandsons, and one great-grandson. Bauman's latest book is *Pranks in Print—A Collection of Fake Stories, Phony Ads, and other Media Mischief*. Learn more about his work at www.richardjbauman.com.

PATRICIA BELOTE is the author of the poetry chapbook, *Traveling Light* (Finishing Line Press). Her recent work appears in *The Healing Muse, U.S. 1 Worksheets, Cumberland River Review, Saw Palm: Florida Literature and Art, Meridian Anthology of Contemporary Poetry*, and *Collected Poems of the Panhandle Poets*. Belote lives along Florida's Gulf Coast and plays Celtic fiddle tunes when she's not writing.

PIERRE-MARIE BERNARD found out quite early in his life that music loved him. He came to that conclusion from the continuous gifts of joy and happiness that she was offering him—every single day and through all kinds of different music styles. He thought he should really do something about it and give some of this love back. Music playing seems like an obvious thing to do but after he failed miserably at every single instrument of the orchestra, he gave up and decided to let play those who are qualified for this activity. To the great relief of his family and neighbors, he decided to switch to a keyboard with letters on it and went on to write stories. At the age of forty-six, this procrastinator by profession, optimist by nature, and French man by chance is putting the final touches on a series of music-inspired short stories that he hopes will find its niche in a currently non-existent market for short-stories books in France.

CHINMOY BISWAS is a school teacher by profession, but is also passionate about photography through which he captures nature and people. Based in India, Biswas regularly participates in photography salons and competitions. He has won numerous awards both nationally and internationally, including the Salon International Photo-phylles (France) 2014 UPI Silver medal and the Sille Sanat Sarayi International Salon (Turkey) FIAP Gold medal in 2015.

MAROULA BLADES is a poet/writer living in Berlin. The winner of the Erbacce Prize 2012, her first poetry collection "Blood Orange" was published by erbacce-press in the United Kingdom. Her works have been published in *Volume Magazine*, *Abridged O-40*, *Trespass Magazine*, *Thrice Fiction Magazine*, *Kaleidoscope*, and by the Latin Heritage Foundation and other anthologies and magazines. Her poetry/music programme has been presented on several stages in Germany. Her debut EP album, *Word Pulse* (Havavision Records) can be found on iTunes and Amazon.

GARY BLOOM grew up in Minneapolis and attended Mankato (Minnesota) State University. His articles, short stories, photography, and poetry have been published in newspapers, magazines, and websites. He currently has poems on www.strongverse.org and www.punchnels.com. After retiring from work as a database administrator, he now spends his time writing and traveling. He lives in Pass Christian, Mississippi.

ALMA H. BOND became a full-time writer when she was sixty-six years old, leaving behind thirty-seven years as a psychoanalyst in New York City. She has published professional articles in prestigious psychoanalytic journals over the years, as well as more than twenty books, including her *On the Couch* series, which explores psychoanalytical insights into the lives of some of the world's most fascinating women such as Hillary Clinton, Marilyn Monroe, Jackie O, and Lady Macbeth. Bond has also published biographies on Michelle Obama and Margaret Mahler, the latter of which received multiple awards, as well as many other books. She wrote the play, *Maria*, about the life and loves of Maria Callas, which was produced off-off Broadway and toured through the South. She is a member of the American Society of Journalists and Authors, the Dramatists Guild, the International Psychoanalytic Association, the Institute for Psychoanalytic Training and Research, and the American Psychological Association.

Bond's late husband, Rudy Bond, was a well-known actor, appearing in many films such as *A Streetcar Named Desire*, top Broadway shows, and in 100 TV plays. He also wrote the book *I Rode A Streetcar Named Desire* about how he came to "land" his powerful role alongside Marlon Brando.

Bond has three children, all of whom have published books of their own, and eight grandchildren, none of whom have published books as of yet. Learn more about Bond and her work at www.almabondauthor.com.

MICHAEL BOOTY is a lifelong music lover who currently resides in Arkansas. When he's not chasing the euphoric intensity of the underground live music scene, he can be found sharing his passion for literature and lyricism with his students at the University of Arkansas Community College in Morrilton.

FRANCISCO PARADO BUENAFE is a photographer based in the Philippines who has explored an array of industries over the course of his career. In addition to working as a photojournalist, he studied preparatory law at Adamson University (Manila) as well as piano and violin at the University of Santo Tomas. He earned a master's degree in electronics from the National Technical School in California as a correspondent student. He designed and erected a lattice communications tower in the Philippines, and while he is now retired, he continues to provide maintenance for this project.

MATT CLARKE is an award-winning wildlife photographer, filmmaker, and music composer from the United Kingdom. Currently assisting Will Burrard-Lucas, one of the world's top wildlife photographers, he also spends much of his time based in Zambia's South Luangwa National Park working with The Bushcamp Company as their photographer and filmmaker. You can learn more about Clarke at www.mattclarkewildlife.com.

BILL CUSHING, a Los Angeles-based poet, is pleased to return to the pages of *Stories of Music*. In addition to being published in Volume 1, his poems have appeared in *Avocet, Brownstone Review, Penumbra, genius & madness*, the *Onion River Review*, the *Synergist, Spectrum*, and the *Sabal Palm Review*. Cushing earned an MFA in writing from Goddard College in Vermont, and now teaches English classes at both Mount San Antonio and East Los Angeles colleges. Because of his involvement in *Stories of Music*, Volume 1, he was able to reconnect with a childhood neighbor, who also now lives in Los Angeles, and the two have begun collaborative performances of poetry and music under the name of "Notes and Letters." Cushing invites anyone interested in the idea (and especially those in the So-Cal area) to join their Facebook page of the same name for updates, posts, and clips.

DARRIN DUFORD is a writer, mapgazer, and jungle rodent connoisseur. He is the author of *Breakfast for Alligators: Quests, Showdowns, and Revelations in the Americas* and *Is There a Hole in the Boat? Tales of Travel in Panama without a Car*, silver medalist in the 2007 Lowell Thomas Travel Journalism Awards. He has written for the *San Francisco Chronicle, BBC Travel, Gastronomica, Roads & Kingdoms, Transitions Abroad*, and *Perceptive Travel*, among others. His work has been anthologized in *The Best Travel Writing, Volume 11* and *Stories of Music*, Volume 1. Follow him on Twitter at @darrinduford.

ELIZABETH ERENBERG is a flutist, teacher, and musical entrepreneur. Her classical training has expanded into collaborations with other genres, performance techniques, and art forms. In 2014, she released *ASCEND*, an album of new music for flute and other instruments. Currently she resides in York, Pennsylvania where she is an active freelancer, recording artist, and teacher. She holds degrees from the University of Oregon and New England Conservatory of Music. Learn more at www.elizabetherenberg.com.

PATRICIA J. ESPOSITO is the author of *Beside the Darker Shore*, and she has published numerous works in anthologies, such as Timbre Press's *Stories of Music*, Volume 1, Main Street Rag's *Crossing Lines*, Cohesion Press's *Blurring the Line*, Annapurna's *Clarify*, and Undertow's *Apparitions*, and in magazines, including *Scarlet Literary Magazine*, *Rose and Thorn*, *Karamu*, *Clean Sheets*, *Wicked Hollow*, and *Midnight Street*. She has received honorable mentions in Ellen Datlow's Year's Best Fantasy and Horror collections and she is a Pushcart Prize nominee.

GARY FEARON is a writer, songwriter, and artist based in the suburbs of Memphis, Tennessee. He is also creative director at *Southern Writers Magazine* where he interviews authors, writes instructional articles, and oversees publication production, websites, and TV and radio advertisements.

LUCY GABRIEL is an English poet, with a secret identity as a speculative fiction writer. She lives with two cats, and a long-suffering husband who doesn't understand why she can't stick to one thing at a time. Her works have appeared, or are due to appear, in *Pantheon Magazine* and the *Tranquility* anthology by Kind of a Hurricane Press. She can be found on Facebook at www.facebook.com/lucygabrielpoet and on Twitter as @lucygabrielpoet.

SHARON GLASSMAN writes and performs stories and songs that explore big ideas in warmhearted ways. Her essays, features, and music appear on public radio, digital radio, and podcasts. She's presented her stage stories about women in science, true love, and the art of giving nationwide.

Glassman lives in northern Colorado, where she creates The Lazy Person's Book Club live shows, podcasts, and audio books. Blackstone Audio recently released her Lazy Person's Book Club audio novel with songs, *Blame It On Hoboken*, featuring the song, "Mulligan Waltz." Say hello and hear more at http://sharonglassmanlive.com.

MARC GOLDIN, born and raised in Chicago, still lives there, working in a nonprofit health clinic near the historic Bronzeville neighborhood. He writes short fiction that has been published in *Deep*

South Magazine and *Crab Fat Magazine*, as well as non-fiction—his piece on the Beats in Tangier was published in an India-based literary journal, *Café Dissensus*. Although he has traveled widely looking for music, his hometown of Chicago has ultimately provided the widest cultural range of anything one would want. He lives with a demanding, one-eyed Persian cat.

STEPHEN GRIGGS is a composer, performer, and writer with two awards from Chamber Music America/ASCAP for Adventurous Programming of Contemporary Music. His musical practice focuses on connecting history, music, and place related to social justice in Seattle. His writing can be found at http://stevegriggsmusic.blogspot.com and his music at http://stevegriggsmusic.com. His writing has been reprinted in *Rhythm in the Rain* (Ooligan Press) and *Creative Colloquy Second Anthology*. Griggs is currently working on a biography of Detroit saxophonist Joe Brazil.

PENNY HARTER is published widely in journals and anthologies, and her literary autobiography appears as an extended essay in *Contemporary Authors*. Her twenty-two books and chapbooks include *The Resonance Around Us* (2013), *One Bowl* (2012), a prizewinning e-chapbook of haibun, *Recycling Starlight* (2010), *The Beastie Book* (2009), an illustrated alphabestiary, and *The Night Marsh* (2008).

Harter was a featured reader at the 2010 Geraldine R. Dodge Poetry Festival, and she has won three poetry fellowships from the New Jersey State Council on the Arts; the Mary Carolyn Davies Award from the Poetry Society of America; the first William O. Douglas Nature Writing Award for her work in the anthology *American Nature Writing: 2002*; and two residencies from the Virginia Center for the Creative Arts (January 2011 and March 2015). Learn more about Harter and her work at www.penhart.wordpress.com and www.2hweb.net/penhart.

KEVIN HAWORTH is a 2016 National Endowment for the Arts fellow and director of the low-residency MFA program at Carlow University in Pittsburgh. His books include the novel *The Discontinuity of Small Things*, the essay collection *Famous Drownings in Literary History*, and the limited edition essay chapbook *Far Out All My Life*. His collection of essays about writing, *Lit from Within: Contemporary Masters on the Art and Craft of Writing*, co-edited with Dinty W. Moore, was recognized as an American Library Association Outstanding Title, as one of *Writer* magazine's Top 10 Writing Books, and featured in *Poets & Writers'* Best Books for Writers List. He has held residencies at Vermont Studio Center, Headlands Center for the Arts, and Ledig International Writers House. He recently participated in "Public Writing, Public Libraries," a public art project, in which his essays were printed on the windows of libraries throughout the state of Iowa.

WILLIAM HUHN's narratives have appeared in *The South Carolina Review*, *Tulane Review*, *Fugue*, *Strings*, and other publications. His work has been twice nominated for a Pushcart Prize and has been cited five times as a "Notable Essay" in *The Best American Essays* series (most recently in 2016). A chapbook of Huhn's poetry was published by Red Dancefloor Press as part of their Prime Poets Series, and his credits include a letter in *The New Yorker* about James Thurber. Huhn and his wife are currently based in New York City, where she dances for the American Liberty Ballet.

CAROLYN T. JOHNSON, a former banker and now freelance writer from Houston, Texas, writes from the heart, the hurt, the heavenly, and sometimes the hilarious. Her work can be found in *Halcyon Days* magazine, the *Houston Chronicle*, and the *Austin American-Statesman* newspapers, as well as in *Chicken Soup for the Soul: O Canada*, Whispering Angel Books' anthologies, Publishing Syndicate books, *Seek It: Writers and Artists Do Sleep*, and numerous other anthologies and e-zines.

ALEKSANDR KUZNETCOV is a professional musician from Russia who graduated from the St. Petersburg Conservatory. In addition to his passion for music he also enjoys photography, particularly photographing other musicians because he understands them very well. Through his photography, Kuznetcov tries to reflect the internal state of his subjects.

MICHAEL LEE is a healer, writer, and actor from New South Wales, Australia. He writes lyrics and poetry, and is a budding screenwriter. His first feature film script, *Our Girl* is currently out to a top producer. Trained in the Body Mirror System of Healing, Lee's latest project is developing content for his new website and business called That Healing Guy (http://thathealingguy.com), with the main focus being to open the hearts of men all over the world. He aims to reach one million people by 2021.

In his down time, he's often at home in Sydney with his sweetheart Tania, where they bring their dream of their very own "Truth Cottage" in the country into their everyday reality.

ZACHARY J. LEE is an English major at the University of Missouri–St. Louis, focusing on creative writing and gender studies. He is a member of the Pierre Laclede Honors College and the University Singers at UMSL. Lee believes deeply in the healing power of music and writing, and is especially interested in the intersection of those two ideas.

DARRELL LINDSEY is the author of *Edge of the Pond* (Popcorn Press 2012), and has been nominated for a Pushcart Prize (2007) and a Rhysling Award (2014). He won the 2012 Science Fiction Poetry

Association Contest (Long Form category), as well as the 2014 Balticon Poetry Contest. His work has appeared in more than sixty journals and anthologies.

HARRY LONGSTREET is retired after twenty-five years as a writer, producer, and director of filmed entertainment, primarily for television. When he's not busy with his wife, children, and grandchildren, he keeps the creative juices flowing with his still photography.

He's always looking for images that speak to the human condition and the world around him. He favors ambient light and unposed, unaware subjects. In the last ten years, he's had a number of one-man shows, and his work has appeared in more than 200 national and international juried exhibitions.

Longstreet is twice a Single Image Merit Award recipient from *Black & White Magazine* and twice a Single Image Merit Award winner from *Color Magazine*. In 2013, he was awarded the Gold Medal (monochrome) in the International Varna Salon, and in 2014, he took Best in Show in the annual CVG (Collective Visions Gallery) Washington State competition. His images have been included in *Creative Quarterly*'s 100 Best in 2014 and 2015.

JOHN MCDONALD, recently described as "the New England master of the short piece" in a recording review, is a composer who tries to play the piano and a pianist who tries to compose. He is a professor of music at Tufts University, where he has served both as music department chair and director of graduate music studies. He teaches composition, theory, and performance at Tufts. His output concentrates on vocal, chamber, and solo instrumental works, and includes interdisciplinary experiments. On sabbatical from Tufts, he is currently completing a biography project on composer T(homas) J(efferson) Anderson. McDonald is also serving as the Joseph E. and Grace W. Valentine Visiting Professor of Music at Amherst College for the 2016-2017 academic year.

JERIN MICHEAL is a press and editorial photographer currently studying at Falmouth University in the South West Coast of England. At age eighteen, he has already won the prestigious NME's Under 18 Music Photographer of the Year and he has also exhibited his work at the Louvre in Paris. His subjects vary from world renowned musicians to deep-sea fishermen. No matter what he turns his lens to, he is enthralled by the story. When he isn't shooting, he enjoys good coffee and bad films. See more of Micheal's work at www.jerinmichealphotography.com.

TRACIE RENEE AMIRANTE PADAL grew up playing the violin and is now a librarian, an award-winning poet, and a member of the TallGrass Writers Guild. Her poems have appeared in anthologies (including *Embers and Flames*, *The Official Poets' Guide to Peace*, and *Stories of Music*, Volume 1), newspapers, magazines, and journals. Most recently, Padal was nominated for a Pushcart Prize. She lives in suburban Chicago.

MUKTA PATIL is a freelance editor and writer based out of Goa, India. Writing is more than a passing interest for her, and she is deeply interested in issues related to the environment, gender, and culture. She can usually be found on the beach, nose buried in a book.

ELENA POLYAKOVA writes about art and entertainment as a professional journalist in Novosibirsk, Siberia. She spends her free time walking around the city as an amateur street photographer.

ROBERT B. ROBESON is a retired US Army Lt. Col. with over twenty-seven years of service on three continents and in combat as a helicopter medical evacuation pilot. He's been decorated for valor eight times. After his military career, he was a newspaper managing editor and columnist. Now as a freelance writer, he's published nearly 900 articles, short stories, and poems in over 320 publications in 130 countries. This includes *Reader's Digest*, *Vietnam Combat*, *Official Karate*, *Writer's Digest*, *Frontier Airline Magazine*, and *Newsday*, among others. His work has also been published in fifty anthologies. He has a Bachelor of Arts degree in English from the University of Maryland-College Park and has completed extensive undergraduate and graduate work in journalism at the University of Nebraska-Lincoln. He's a professional (life) member of the National Writers Association, the Veterans of Foreign Wars, the Dustoff Association, and the Distinguished Flying Cross Society.

KENNETH SALZMANN is a writer and poet whose work has appeared in such anthologies as *Child of My Child: Poems and Stories for Grandparents* (Gelles-Cole Literary Enterprises), *Beloved on the Earth: 150 Poems of Grief and Gratitude* (Holy Cow! Press), *Riverine: An Anthology of Hudson Valley Writers* (Codhill Press), *Earth Blessings* (Viva Editions), and *Stories of Music*, Volume 1 (Timbre Press). He lives in Woodstock, New York, and Ajijic, Mexico, with his wife, editor Sandi Gelles-Cole.

JEFF SANTOSUOSSO is a business consultant and poet living in Pensacola, Florida. A member of the Florida State Poets Association, he is co-editor of panoplyzine.com, an online journal dedicated to poetry and short prose. His work has been nominated for a Pushcart Prize and has appeared in *San Pedro River Review*, *Illya's Honey*, *Red River Review*, *Texas Poetry Calendar* (2012, 2014), *Avocet*, *Red Fez*, *Alalit*, *Extract(s)*, *First Literary Review-East*, and other online and print publications. You can find him on Facebook at www.facebook.com/jeff.santosuosso.

BAR SCOTT is a singer-songwriter and writer who leads writing workshops in both Colorado and New York. She has published over sixty-five songs, a memoir, *The Present Giver*, a workbook for writers called *The Lone Writer's Writing Club*, and two short pieces in *The Sun* magazine called "Tight Spot" and "Breasts." Her story "Grace" was included in *Stories of Music*, Volume 1. Learn more about her work at www.barscott.com.

PHILIP SEE is a musician from Seattle, Washington who was diagnosed with multiple sclerosis in 2002, and lost his ability to play music shortly thereafter. With persistence, he was able to regain his musical ability through neuroplasticity. Passionate about helping other musicians with neurological disorders regain their musical abilities as well, See now leads a free program called Get Back Your Music at Seattle's Multiple Sclerosis Center at Swedish Medical Center. Through this program, he organizes one-on-one and group "jam sessions" that focus on reconditioning the participants' affected areas. Learn more about Get Back Your Music at www.swedish.org/services/neuroscience-institute/our-services/multiple-sclerosis-center/comprehensive-wellness/physical-wellness/rehabilitation-and-fitness/wellness-and-exercise-classes.

RUSSELL STEINBERG is a composer who received a PhD in music from Harvard University, an MM from the New England Conservatory, and a BA from UCLA. Performances of his solo, chamber, and orchestral music recently included concerts in Los Angeles, Baltimore, New Jersey, Vienna, and Prague. "Aria for a Calmer World" (violin and orchestra) was featured in the San Bernardino Cares benefit concert for the families of the victims of the 2015 terrorist attack. For the twenty-fifth anniversary of the Hubble Space Telescope, "Cosmic Dust" (commissioned by a tri-consortium of orchestras—the New West Symphony, the Bay Atlantic Symphony, and the Hopkins Symphony) was featured in a special *Science News Magazine* article and was performed for the Hubble scientists. The Los Angeles Jewish Symphony recently premiered *Canopy of Peace* based on meditations by noted scholar and philosopher Rabbi Harold M. Schulweis. Available recordings of Steinberg's music include *Sacred Transitions: A Song Cycle Based On Meditations by Harold M. Schulweis, Stories from My Favorite Planet: A Musical Tribute to Journalist Daniel Pearl* produced by the Daniel Pearl Foundation, *Flute Sonata* on Centaur Records recorded by Michelle Stanley, *Desert Stars*, Steinberg's solo music for piano and classical guitar, and "Fantasy for Flute and Piano" on the album *ASCEND* featuring flutist Elizabeth Erenberg. For information about Steinberg's current performances, recordings, and pre-concert lectures, please visit www.russellsteinberg.com.

KELLY J. STIGLIANO has been consistently writing for weekly newspapers since the 1990s. Her articles have been published in *Guideposts, War Cry, Pentecostal Evangel*, Focus on the Family's *Clubhouse*

Magazine, Just Between Us, Sasee, Cross & Quill, Christian Communicator magazines, and more. Her articles have appeared on websites such as CBN.com, Charismamag.com, and ThrivingFamily.com, and she is a blogger for Mentoring Moments for Christian Women. Her stories have been included in eleven compilation books including *Chicken Soup for the Soul*, two *Guideposts* series, two Cecil Murphey books, and *Love Is a Verb Devotional* by Gary Chapman. She has enjoyed speaking to women's groups, teenagers, and teachers since 1987, and currently speaks throughout the southeastern USA. She is also a member of Word Weavers International writers' critique group. Learn more about her work at www.kellystigliano.com.

ELIZABETH KIRKPATRICK VRENIOS' poetry has appeared in *Clementine*, Silver Birch Press anthologies, *Kentucky Review, Bethlehem Writers Roundtable, Poeming Pigeon, Form Quarterly, The Edison Literary Review*, and *Unsplendid*. She was a 30/30 poet for Tupelo Press, and her prize-winning chapbook, *Special Delivery*, was published by Yellow Chair Press. She also co-wrote the book *Party Line* under the name Elizabeth Kirkpatrick. Vrenios is a professor emerita from American University in Washington D.C., having chaired the vocal and music departments. Vrenios' solo recitals throughout the United States, South America, Scandinavia, Japan, and Europe have been acclaimed, and as the artistic director of the Redwoods Opera Workshop in Mendocino, California and the Crittenden Opera Workshops in Washington D.C. and Boston, she has influenced and trained students across the country. She is a member of the International Who's Who of Music and a past president of the National Opera Association.